Tuning In to
GOD'S
CALL

Andrew Carl Wisdom, OP *(signature)*

Andrew Carl Wisdom, OP
and Christine Kiley, ASCJ

FOREWORD BY
The Most Reverend Edward M. Rice
Auxiliary Bishop of St. Louis

To Diane,
God will reward you
richly for being my sister's
friend and my loyal supporter.
☺

Liguori
ONE LIGUORI DRIVE
LIGUORI MO 63057-9999

Imprimi Potest:
Harry Grile, CSsR, Provincial
Denver Province, The Redemptorists

Published by Liguori Publications, Liguori, Missouri 63057
To order, call 800-325-9521, or visit liguori.org.

Library of Congress Cataloging-in-Publication Data

Wisdom, Andrew Carl, 1961-
    Tuning in to God's call / Andrew Carl Wisdom and Christine Kiley.—1st ed.
        p. cm.
    ISBN 978-0-7648-2140-0
    1. Discernment (Christian theology)—Prayers and devotions. 2. Listening—
Religious aspects—Christianity—Prayers and devotions. I. Kiley, Christine. II. Title.
    BV4509.5.W57 2012
    248.4—dc23

                                                                                    2012010655

Printed in the United States of America
16 15 14 13 12 / 5 4 3 2 1
First Edition

Dedication

We gratefully dedicate this work to those with whom we first discerned a vocation.

THE WISDOM AND KILEY FAMILIES

We also dedicate *Tuning In to God's Call* to:

— the many young men and women with whom we had the privilege to help discern their vocations, some of whom we joyfully call our religious brothers or sisters today.

— the Dominican Friars of the Central Province of St. Albert the Great and the Apostles of the Sacred Heart of Jesus, U.S. Province, who daily inspire us to live fully the beauty and blessing of our vocations.

Contents

Contents

Part V: Signs of a Good Discernment 94

Foreword

When I was a junior in high school, I first began to open my heart to a vocation to the priesthood. I had no idea what to do with my thoughts, and I felt I had no one to turn to. Luckily I brought it up with my guidance counselor.

It was not long after that I received information about our diocesan seminary, and I was filling out the application. As I look back on the process, it all seemed so simple.

Today our young people have technology at their fingertips and can communicate in ways that did not exist back then. Today they can send a message halfway round the world within seconds or post personal thoughts for all to see. Yet for all the ability to communicate, there is a price. We can lack the face-to-face encounter with another human being. The very technology that assists us in communicating can cause alienation and lead some to withdraw. Our dependence on the computer can hinder our ability to form mature relationships.

The *Catechism of the Catholic Church* reminds us that God desires to communicate with us: "The desire for God is written in the human heart...and God never ceases to draw man to himself" (*CCC* 27). With *Tuning In to God's Call*, Sister Christine Kiley, ACSJ, and Father Andrew Carl Wisdom, OP, offer the young people of our Church a valuable tool for getting in touch with the human heart and the stirrings of God. The book's general format of Scripture, reflection, quote, action, and prayer will assist the reader in fostering a relationship with the living God. The authors' choice of a "low-tech" method of prayer and reflection reminds us that, ultimately, when one opens the heart to the will of God, one discovers a "vital and personal relationship with the living and true God" (*CCC* 2558).

Sometimes we must disconnect in order to reconnect. This certainly applies to discovering one's vocation. The reflections and the format outlined in this book will assist young people in discerning the will of God in the depths of their hearts. By reading *Tuning In to God's Call*, readers will discover what the title character in *Alice's Adventures in Wonderland* was looking for when she asked the Cheshire Cat, "Would you tell me, please, which way I ought to go from here?"

THE MOST REVEREND EDWARD M. RICE
AUXILIARY BISHOP OF ST. LOUIS

Introduction

When Alice in the popular children's book *Alice's Adventures in Wonderland* meets the Cheshire Cat, she asks him, "Would you tell me, please, which way I ought to go from here?" He responds, "That depends a good deal on where you want to get to." Alice answers, "I don't much care where." "Then," the Cat says, "it doesn't matter which way you go."

Discernment is about getting somewhere. And it does matter which way you go. It has a beginning point and an end point. But before you can know which way to go, you have to know where you want to "get to." What is the goal of your search? If, as a Christian, your goal is to know the will of God for your life, then that is where you begin: with the end in sight! Observing, as Father Thomas Dubay did, that acorns grow into oak trees, tadpoles into frogs, and babies into adults, so Christians are to grow into an *alter Christus*, another Christ. How do we know if we are becoming that fully mature man or woman in Christ? More precisely, how do we know where we are in the process of that becoming? What vocational expression should it take in my life: marriage, the single life, religious life, or priesthood?

For the Christian, discernment is both interior and exterior. It requires steadfastness in prayer that enables you to be attuned daily to the voice of God in life. God speaks to us through the events, experiences, and encounters that make up each day.

We respond by following that inner voice with concrete action that reflects its direction. The fruit of discernment is decision.

That's where we, the authors, come in. Like the Cheshire Cat, we want to help you "get to" where you are going. This means assisting and providing guidance that walks with you as you discover your life's call. This is not a book about discernment, but rather it discerns alongside you. Consider us your spiritual companions—those who will walk with you on your spiritual journey. Through the reflections in these pages, we hope to help you understand where you are on the path of following God's will for your life.

Please treat this book as a blueprint of the various building blocks of discernment. Knowing how these blocks of discernment will help you along the way is crucial. If attended to, they will keep you at your task and help you to be accountable to yourself and God for the most important mission of your life: how to become his "other Christ" in the world.

Sometimes the obstacles we find in discernment—the blocks that don't seem to build toward a decision but cause us to stumble—are mere disguises for invitations to see things in a new way. What is the pattern of divine love in my life, and what is God's love inviting me to do? How do we recognize the grace of God at work in our minds and hearts? How is God working in this event, in this encounter, in this effort at hand? What do my spiritual experiences, my prayer life, and my relationship with God tell me about my life choice? These are precisely what the spiritual companion points out and helps to bring to our awareness in this process we call discernment.

Our hope in accompanying you in your discernment is to inspire, challenge, and ultimately encourage you to keep moving forward even when the road gets tough. While our Lord does say: "It was not you who chose me, but I who chose you" (John 15:16), he will not do all the work for us. God respects our freedom too much! With the gift of life comes free will. Free will means: Decide. God will be there to provide us with grace and strength each step of the way. It is that divine grace and strength that will help us find and choose that which is ultimately choosing us.

In the long run, a vocation, whether to the married or single life, ordained or religious life, is less our story than God's. In these pages, may you discover the unfolding of your own story in the larger arms of God's story.

PART I

What Is Discernment?

"Eternal God, eternal Trinity...I desire above all to see you, the true light, as you really are."

SAINT CATHERINE OF SIENA

DISCERNMENT is a process whereby we seek to discover God's presence and action in our lives. Before making a decision, we intentionally stop to consider and reflect upon how our desires match what God wants for us. The goal of discernment is to discover God's personal and wholly unique call to us, to me. As a person claimed by Christ in baptism, we believe God is always at work in us and that we are called to be the Lord's instrument in the world. How God calls me to be that instrument is the stuff of discernment.

The Church invites all to make a generous gift of one's life to God either through marriage, an intentional single life, the priesthood, or religious life. Which of these vocational choices represents the most generous gift of our self, not objectively, but subjectively? God wants us to not merely survive in our life choices, but—in accordance with Saint Thomas Aquinas' thought—God wants our human flourishing. In what calling, although sometimes challenging, would one most flourish?

WAKING UP

SCRIPTURE: "I was sleeping, but my heart was awake."

SONG OF SONGS 5:2

REFLECTION: Have you ever considered that so many of us go through this world as though asleep at the wheel of our lives? Yet our hearts lie awake with a gnawing hunger, an all-consuming thirst not easily quenched. This abiding hunger and thirst is actually a gift that, when fully acknowledged, awakens our whole being and compels us to go deeper, to seek after the *more*. How often have we glimpsed this thirst in ourselves and other people when they lament: *There has to be something more. This can't be all there is.* Indeed, these moments are a wake-up call from God to go deeper. There is a *more* to go to, and God nudges us toward it. That *more* is what gives our life its ultimate meaning and centers us in our truest identity.

When I was in the business world, the reaction of those who learned of my decision to leave my career and become a Dominican priest struck me. My co-workers commented: "It must be nice to know your meaning in life." This is "the *more*" that speaks to our deepest hunger and allows us to live a life fully awake: knowing with every fiber of one's being that meaning in life does not come from our roles and responsibilities but from our eternal identity as God's beloved children.

Now go through this day, awake to the reality that beyond mother or father, Republican or Democrat, businesswoman or janitor, your deepest identity—the one before all others—is an identity as God's beloved, the dignity of which no one and nothing can take away.

QUOTE: *"Savior, your divine plan for the world is a mirror for the spiritual world; teach us to walk in the world as spiritual men [and women]."*

SAINT EPHREM

ACTION: Make a quick list of your top five priorities. Are they reflective of what you find most meaningful in life, what you truly hunger for, or rather how you define yourself before others?

PRAYER: Tender God, this is your beloved child. I was asleep, but you have awakened my heart, and now my heart in your heart is awakening the rest of me to the truth of my identity in you. Help me to go about this day knowing my dignity as your very own beloved son or daughter.

ADSUM

SCRIPTURE: "Mary said, 'Behold, I am the handmaid of the Lord. May it be done to me according to your word.'"

LUKE 1:38

REFLECTION: Mary, the Mother of God, has always been the epitome of openness and God-centeredness for all women and men. Her "yes" to God changed human history. At an art exhibit by Holly Schapker, who inspiringly captured the life and work of Saint Ignatius of Loyola in paint and textiles, this short introduction to her collection speaks clearly to the message and disposition needed for discernment:

"On the night Gabriel visited Mary, as the biblical passage goes, he asked her to bear a child who would be called Emmanuel, a name that means **"God is with us.**" *Perhaps there was a pause until she answered,* "Adsum," *which is the Latin expression for* **"I am here.**" *Not a word easily translated into the English language,* Adsum *means being in a state of mind where the person is completely available and willing to serve God. The Spiritual Exercises of Saint Ignatius allowed me to approach this state in my painting studio and outside of it."*

HOLLY SCHAPKER

Being in a state of mind where the person is completely available and willing to serve God is the state of mind, heart, and soul for which we pray in the discernment process.

QUOTE: *"There are very few people who realize what God would make of them if they abandoned themselves into his hands and let God form them by his grace."*

IGNATIUS OF LOYOLA, SJ

ACTION: Can you imagine the many ways that you can be available, open, and willing to serve Jesus Christ? Make known to the Lord all of your feelings, hopes, dreams, and plans that come to mind.

PRAYER: My Redeemer, I feel within the depths of my being a great desire to be completely available to know you, to love you, to serve you. This desire must be a gift of your grace because it has come to me as a complete surprise, and it gives me great peace.

DISCERNMENT

SCRIPTURE: "The harvest is abundant but the laborers are few."
MATTHEW 9:37

REFLECTION: Are you struggling with important decisions in your life? Are you searching for a way to sort out and prioritize your options, opportunities, or to find a path of resolution with which you are content? This is discernment and the work of one who is discerning.

Discernment is not a straightforward, step-by-step process but an approach that will lead you to a place of peace with your most important decisions. Whether it is about a career or college choice, a relationship, or a life decision—your goal is to process information with openness and weigh your options in order to choose the best path before you.

Begin with a prayer. Teresa of Ávila speaks about prayer as a heart-to-heart conversation with the One who knows and loves you. Relationship with God is crucial as you make decisions, and a loving conversation with God is a necessity.

Clear discernment will also require research. This is like trying on new clothes to see what fits best. What is comfortable or what feels like something that is compatible with your personality? Check out and attend to the particulars of these choices. If it is a serious life choice, then speak with a counselor, a family member, or a trusted friend to further discern this option. Writing out the pros and cons and many aspects of the choices before you might be a clarifying action.

Important decisions are never easy to make and should not be taken lightly.

Perhaps you have prayed faithfully for months or sometimes even for years and researched, consulted, and gathered information. It is natural to feel confused and bewildered from time to time. "How," you ask, "am I going to narrow this down and make any sense of what to do with my life?"

Relax! Jesus never said it would be easy, but he did say: "Behold, I am with you always, until the end of the age" (Matthew 28:20). Wise mentors and objective friends are critical to the process. Trust is vital: Trust God, others, and your inner self as you think, pray, and feel your way forward and prepare to make the decisions before you. Recognize that you are the only one who can decide, and God gives you full freedom to discern and choose the path before you. Do not be afraid!

QUOTE: *"Once the love of God has released him from self-love, the flame of divine love never ceases to burn in his heart and he remains united to God by an irresistible longing."*

DIADOCHUS OF PHOTICE

ACTION: List the ways that you can (1) trust more today and (2) remain in the truth.

PRAYER: Come, Spirit of God, teach me your ways. Continue to guide me with your tender hand. Show me where to seek, to knock, and to ask with trust.

THE THREE CALLS

SCRIPTURE: "Blessed are those who dwell in your house! O LORD of hosts, blessed the man who trusts in you!"

PSALM 84:5, 13

REFLECTION: Connie burst into the Campus Ministry office: "I just had a lightning-bolt experience! I saw that film on Mother Teresa and thought: *I want to give my life to the poor and help others, and I know that this is something I can do, want to do, and will do.* I remember thinking this same thought when I made my first Communion and again when I was confirmed. The bishop said that some in the class were called to be religious and priests, and in my heart I felt a strong call accompanied by a feeling of peace and joy! This same feeling returned tonight after the movie."

This is a call from God that is considered unusual. It is much like the man who sees someone across a crowded room and is clear that this is the person he will one day marry. These moments, though rare, have proven successful and are beautiful illustrations of how God fulfills lives. A call like this one should still be discerned: examined, researched, and questioned before a decision is made to move forward.

Another more common type of call is *vocation by attraction.* A person experiences a grace-filled inspiration through another person, event, dream, interest, or desire. One may be drawn over time to a specific mission, ministry or way of serving God in religious life or the priesthood. The call is sustained through thick and thin. Struggles and temptations may be a real part of the search for the truth of where one is best suited to serve God and attain salvation. Yet with direction, prayer, and soul-searching, a person moves toward a peaceful resolution and decision.

A third type of call is *vocation by reason*. In this call, the person is moved intellectually and with her eyes on God; she tends to search for the answer with an analytical bent. Saint Ignatius recommends a logical process for this discerner.

Each of these ways that God calls have some overlapping experiences, and each call is—in a sense—unique. The life call of each of us is written in the heart of God and is beyond any script we could have imagined or dreamed for ourselves. We look at God's way of mapping our lives and pray for the grace to respond to both small and large calls each day with a resounding YES!

QUOTE: *"God visits us with so many lights, with so many inspirations of his grace."*

MOTHER CLELIA MERLONI
SERVANT OF GOD

ACTION: Sit in silent adoration before the Holy Eucharist. Place your desires on the altar, asking God to shed light on your decisions and help you respond to the Lord's call.

PRAYER: Lord, teach us the mysteries of love. I want to choose the life that draws love from me and spend my life serving your people.

BUILDING OUR SPIRITUAL MUSCLES

SCRIPTURE: "Therefore, since we are surrounded by so great a cloud of witnesses, let us rid ourselves of every burden and sin that clings to us and persevere in running the race that lies before us while keeping our eyes fixed on Jesus, the leader and perfecter of faith."

HEBREWS 12:1–2

REFLECTION: Last year—as an "old guy" of 49—I did something I didn't know I could do: I ran a marathon for the first time. Believe me, along the way I wondered what I had gotten myself into, especially as I neared mile twenty-one of the twenty-six-mile race and felt as if I was going to keel over and see my Creator and Redeemer before my time! But I not only persevered to make it over that finish line, I was able to do it in four hours, forty-five minutes and eight seconds. Not bad, eh?! What made the difference in my doing better than I had ever expected? It was putting everything I had mentally, physically and—especially—spiritually, into the sixteen-week training and trusting the program.

In many ways, every period of discernment for a major decision in Christian life comes disguised as the same opportunity: a training program to strengthen and build our spiritual lungs. This training breathes new life into our capacity to exercise the theological virtues of faith, hope, and love and seek God's will at a particular juncture of our lives. These are not only theological virtues but spiritual muscles within the body of Christ (of which we are a member) that must be further developed or they atrophy. If you don't exercise your faith, you lose it. If you don't practice love, it leaves you. If you don't work out hope, it dies like so much dead muscle tissue. Without these muscles of discernment being disciplined and strengthened, we can't effectively unite our will to God's, which is always the goal of the athlete of Christ.

QUOTE: *"Dear [Brothers and Sisters], we must endure and persevere if we are to attain the truth and freedom we have been allowed to hope for; faith and hope are the very meaning of our being Christians, but if faith and hope are to bear their fruit, patience is necessary."*

SAINT CYPRIAN

ACTION: This week, exercise your spiritual muscles of faith, hope, and love. Make a loving gesture to someone you find difficult to love, a faith witness to someone struggling in his or her beliefs. Encourage someone who has lost hope.

PRAYER: Jesus, my master, teacher, and brother, give me the patience and discipline to train for the only race that matters… the race of faith. Help me to work out the stiff muscles of faith, hope, and love. For through them I become you.

LIFE LIVED TO THE FULL

SCRIPTURE: "I came so that they might have life and have it more abundantly."

JOHN 10:10

REFLECTION: A common fear of many Catholic parents today is that one day a son or daughter will announce his or her desire to enter the seminary or religious life. This fear has been in expressed in many ways. The responses of families range widely: "Why would you do something stupid like that?" Or, "I am not thrilled with the idea, but if that is what you think you want, I will not stop you." My all-time favorite parental response to date is: "You are my kid, but you are God's kid first!" How is that for giving back to God the gift of a son or daughter? The Gospel writer tells us: "Without cost you have received; without cost you are to give" (Matthew 10:8).

Some of the more common responses of recent years include:

"That way of life is for people who cannot find a man [or woman]."

"Lock yourself up in a convent? Isn't that medieval?"

"What a waste of your talents."

"Why would anyone want to do that? That is for someone else's daughter [or son]."

"I always knew that you would do something different for the Church."

"I had a feeling something like that would attract you!"

Life experience has confirmed the conviction that each one

of these comments can be countered with some wonderful life stories of sisters who have lived full, holy, and challenging lives far beyond anything they could have asked for, imagined, or dreamed. Adventures in mission, opportunities for ministry, advanced degrees and travel to the four corners of the world have far surpassed many people's dreams for a life lived "to the full."

QUOTE: *"Not a single day will be without its grace and salvation and its joy."*

POPE JOHN XXIII (LETTER TO HIS NIECE, ENRICA, SEPTEMBER 3, 1955)

ACTIONS: Reflect on the many gifts that God has given you to show Christ to others —to build up the reign of God. Also, journal with the question: Where is fullness of life revealed to me in this place?

PRAYER: Lord Jesus, help me to live in the light of your fullness.

GO, YOU ARE SENT

SCRIPTURE: "You duped me, O Lord and I let myself be duped; you were too strong for me, and you triumphed…I say to myself I will not mention him. I will speak in his name no more. But then it becomes like fire burning in my heart, imprisoned in my bones; I grow weary holding it in, I cannot endure it."

JEREMIAH 20:7, 9

REFLECTION: Christian vocation is rooted in Christ and his invitation again and again to "follow me" (Matthew 4:19) and, "Come, and you will see" (John 1:39). He continually invites people to believe and find their life in him, and when this occurs we are invited to fully live in Christ and are sent forth as a light for the world to see.

Christian vocation is always tied to mission. Jesus himself is called and sent by the Father. His whole life, in fact, is a response. We are called to live out our life with the same generosity of response. No one in the Bible is ever given an experience of God without being sent out. Abraham, Moses, Ruth, Isaiah, Jeremiah, Saul, Mary, the Twelve Apostles, were all called not simply for themselves, but to be sent out on mission. If you notice, the same thing happens at the end of every Eucharist. The final words of the priest are, *Ite missa est*: Go, you are sent forth!

QUOTE: *"Strive with all your power and zeal to be open. With the help of God, try to receive such good counsel that, led solely by the love of God and an eagerness to save souls, you may fulfill your charge."*

SAINT ANGELA MERICI

ACTION: Act as a man or woman sent forth today by Christ. Look for the opportunity to talk with at least two people about your faith, sharing openly about your relationship with the Lord and its impact on discerning your life's direction.

PRAYER: God of the unexpected, give me the courage to take the road less traveled. Break through my resistance and overpower me with your overwhelming love that I might burn with zeal to spread your name everywhere I go, especially where you send me.

COME FOR THE RIDE

SCRIPTURE: "The winding roads shall be made straight and the rough ways smooth."

LUKE 3:5B

REFLECTION: I woke up before dawn, jumped into my sweats and lugged the bike into the van. In a flash I was off to Tower Grove for a Sunday morning ride in the park. What an exhilarating feeling—the gentle October breeze, the breathtaking sunrise, the colorful trees. This is the only way to begin the Sabbath, I thought—space, sun, and solitude.

I rode around the first bend and I prayed for protection from the strangers and safety for the other walkers, runners, and fellow cyclists! Seeing someone approaching with a dog, I tried to reach for the brakes, lost focus and toppled on the curb. I recalled something my dad said when I had a clumsy fall: "The only thing you hurt, Sweetie, was your pride."

Regaining composure and up again for my second lap, my heart swelled with gratitude for the day, its beauty and—this time—solitude. One last turn on my Sunday ride found me glancing down at the chain that seemed to be rubbing on my sneaker—the chain was gradually dropping down and so was the bike. Picking myself up, I still had some distance to go to reach the van. The chain adjusted into place with some effort, leaving my hands greasy. I headed back to the starting point.

Discernment is like a ride in the park! It can be bumpy, most roads have twists and turns—some planned, some unexpected—and occasionally you'll take a spill on the curb. We are not always promised a straight and smooth road, but we can trust in faith that God is along for the ride with us!

–BY C.K.

QUOTE: *"Let us then follow Christ's path which he has revealed to us."*

SAINT AUGUSTINE

ACTION: Journal about an exercise that reflects a stage in your life journey.

PRAYER: Good and gracious God, I pray for the vision to see the road clearly and to navigate the twists and bumps on this road, knowing that the way may become clear when I trust in your plan.

BE ON THE LOOKOUT FOR GOD

SCRIPTURE: "For in one Spirit we were all baptized into one body.... Now the body is not a single part, but many. If a foot should say, 'Because I am not a hand, I do not belong to the body,' it does not for this reason belong any less to the body....God placed the parts, each one of them, in the body as he intended."

1 CORINTHIANS 12:13–15, 18

REFLECTION: One fall, my six-year-old nephew Alex's teacher asked the students to answer the question: "What did I do on my summer vacation?" When Alex's turn came, he stood up and announced to the entire class: "I've been to heaven and I've seen God!"

Alex had just been on his first plane trip. Of course, he believed what his parents had told him, that God lived above the clouds. When the plane ascended above those billowing, white pillows, Alex enthusiastically proclaimed to the entire plane: "We're in heaven; be on the lookout for God!" When the teacher and students seemed slightly skeptical of his experience, Alex folded his arms, looked them in the eye and declared: "My uncle believes me, and he works for God!"

The truth is we all "work" for God by virtue of our baptism. We are all called to become holy and bring that holiness to the world through a particular vocational context. For my sister, Barb, a single woman, that sacred context was to remain intentionally free and available to however Christ wanted to use her in this moment of her life. Putting her Christian discipleship first, she felt called to reach out to economically disadvantaged women and to take them into her home until they got back on their feet. She also spent some time in Indonesia as a lay missionary, and she has served in an ongoing role as a leader for weekly Bible studies.

What is that context for you to do God's work? Alex offers a clue: "Be on the lookout for God" in the experiences and encounters of your day. These events reveal how we should use these encounters to build the reign of God here and now.

QUOTE: *"You are a mystery as deep as the sea; the more I search, the more I find, the more I find, the more I search for you."*

SAINT CATHERINE OF SIENA

ACTION: With pen and paper, recount the day's events and interactions. Mark those in which you were clearly aware of God's grace working though you or another. Jot down what God was saying to or through you.

PRAYER: Tender God, it is almost more than I can believe: You want my help in your holy work to make the kingdom a reality here and now. Give me the generous presence of mind today to be on the lookout for you. Gift me with the wisdom to see how you consistently use me that I might recognize the unfolding of my life's vocation.

CAREER OR CALL?

SCRIPTURE: "I am convinced that neither death, nor life, nor present things or future things, nor powers, nor height, nor depth, nor any other creature will be able to separate us from the love of God in Christ Jesus."

ROMANS 8:38–39

REFLECTION: Career, NO! A call, YES! The culture is very taken by career. Some common questions are: "What are you going to do when you finish college? Go to school, graduate, get a job, get married, have a family and give your parents grand-children? Where will you work? How much money will you make?" Isn't that the normal, typical plan? It is no surprise then, that when a young adult breaks this pattern and decides to consider a call to the priesthood or consecrated life the first questions start.

A call to love Christ as my spouse is not about "doing" but rather about "being." By being a spouse of Christ, people are being all they can be, with their whole heart and soul. If cancer visits us tomorrow it will not much matter what I've been doing. Who we are is far more important.

There is a beautiful reading from the liturgy of the Profession of a Religious where the professed vows to be God's forever and hear Yahweh's voice from the Song of Songs: "Arise my beloved, my beautiful one, and come," (Song of Songs 2:13). In some mysterious way God allows the call to be heard. The precious, priceless YES to God, as Mary echoed at the annunciation, is a single-hearted response that can only emanate from the depth of one's heart. The sacrificial love of vowed life is renewed daily at the Eucharist, where we are invited to receive Christ and then carry him to the world. This awesome call is not a career—it is a way of life! Once people understand this distinction, the call becomes less of a burden to understand, enabling one to accept and embrace a life for God.

QUOTE: *"Open your heart so that the word of God may enter it, take root in it, and bear fruit there for eternal life."*

SAINT FRANCIS DE SALES

ACTION: Just for today try to abandon the habits of technology—e-mail, social networks, your phone, and the connections at your fingertips in order to quiet your spirit and listen for the voice of God. Connect with the eternal and live today for God alone!

PRAYER: Lord God, help us to be tuned in to your call. I want to hear your requests, but the events of the day and distractions sometimes block out your voice. Come and open our hearts!

THE INBUILT DESIGN OF LOVE

SCRIPTURE: "Fear not, O land, delight and rejoice...for the wilderness pastures sprout green grass. The trees bear fruit, the fig tree and the vine produce their harvest....delight and rejoice in the LORD your God! For he has faithfully given you the early rain, sending rain down on you...."

JOEL 2:21–23

REFLECTION: In The Pastoral Constitution on the Church in the Modern World (*Gaudium et Spes*), the Church explains that "here then is the norm for human activity—to harmonize with the authentic interests of the human race, in accordance with God's will and design, and to enable people as individuals and as members of society to pursue and fulfill their total vocation" (*GS* 35).

Just as there is an inbuilt order to nature, God also has an inbuilt design of love and truth for our destiny. We need not be afraid, but rejoice. For just as nature continues to bear fruit according to its design, and just as the rains are there to nurture its roots, so God will give each one of us what we need through the teacher of justice. Justice in the biblical sense is not each one getting his or her due; rather it is right relationship with God and others. Just as nature is in right relationship with God and fulfills its destiny, so God shows us the way to be in right relationship through our life's vocation. The means to this way can be found in Christ Jesus, our teacher of justice.

QUOTE: *"You wanted us to love you, then, we who could not with justice have been saved had we not loved you, nor could we have loved you except by your gift...thus we hold you dear by the affection you have implanted in us."*

WILLIAM OF SAINT THIERRY

ACTION: Take an inventory of your life. Do your priorities give rise to right relationship with the Christ, the teacher of justice? How do your priorities enhance or hinder the discovery of your vocation?

PRAYER: Teacher of Justice, give us the courage to "right" those things in our life that need righting. Help me to trust the ways and means of my life to you. For in you, my fears are powerless and my joys assured.

BUILDING THE REIGN OF GOD

SCRIPTURE: "You turn humanity back into dust, saying, 'Return, you children of Adam!' A thousand years in your eyes are merely a day gone by, before a watch passes in the night, you wash them away; they sleep, and in the morning they sprout again like an herb. In the morning it blooms only to pass away; in the evening it is wilted and withered."

PSALM 90:3–6

REFLECTION: In a business seminar, the presenter began with this startling statement, "It is human arrogance to think you will be here five minutes from now." Most people do not know they are going to die five minutes before they do. Though this may seem to be a depressing reality, this truth is the fuel of our motivation to make each moment in life count.

Our life is lived between the bookends of two biological realities: birth and death. Our response to this limited, precious gift of life is the central question of our existence. In fact, the most important thing about us is not how we look, how much money we can make or even how many friends we have, but that each one of us exists within a wider plan, a grand divine drama likened to an intricately designed mosaic.

We do not exist independent of that wider design but are given the awesome choice and responsibility of cooperating with the Weaver in stitching together our part in the sacred drama. By assuming our unique role, we build the reign of God here and now, in this place, among these circumstances and the people of our lives.

QUOTE: *"So we should at long last rouse ourselves…our eyes should be open to the God-given light, and we should listen in wonderment to the message of the divine voice as it daily cries out… Hurry, while you have the light of life, so that death's darkness may not overtake you."*

SAINT BENEDICT

ACTION: Take ten minutes today to sit before a crucifix and reflect upon the meaning of death as the wellspring to life. Ask yourself what you want your life to have meant when death comes. What do you want others to say was your life's legacy?

PRAYER: Loving Father, remind me to appreciate the fragility of life and to value every moment you give me, wasting not one opportunity to serve you with the precious but limited gift of my existence. Show me the part I am to play in your grand design so that I can make the difference that you intend for me to make.

SHARING IN DIVINE FRIENDSHIP

SCRIPTURE: "It was not you who chose me, but I who chose you and appointed you to go and bear fruit that will remain, so that whatever you ask the Father in my name he may give you."

JOHN 15:16

REFLECTION: The legendary poet T.S. Eliot made famous the idea that at the end of all our discernment in life, we come full circle to the place we began and see and appreciate it as though we had only just arrived. Where we started from is being chosen. We were given the gift of life out of God's love for us. The Creator knit us in our mother's womb and designed everything about us. Yahweh destined us to share in divine friendship and to bring others to that friendship in the unique vocation set forth for each of us. We choose how to respond to God's generosity and love. Our life's challenge is to find the courage to fully choose what has chosen us.

QUOTE: *"If Christ Jesus dwells in a man [or woman] as [a] friend and noble leader, that [person] can endure all things, for Christ helps and strengthens us....What more do we desire from such a good friend at our side? Unlike our friends in the world, he will never abandon us when we are troubled or distressed. Blessed is the one who truly loves him and always keeps him near."*

SAINT TERESA OF ÁVILA

ACTION: Talk to two people today about what they think are your gifts and talents and how you might use them to make a difference for the building of God's kingdom in the world.

PRAYER: Lord God, help me to accept being chosen. Most of all, help me to trust that you know me better than I know myself. With firm faith, may I step forward with confidence and assume the part that is mine to play in your work of gathering all into one.

PART II

Why Should
a Person Discern?

"To love God is the greatest of all romances; to seek him, the greatest adventure; to find him, the greatest human achievement."

SAINT AUGUSTINE OF HIPPO

"Those whom God calls must answer his call in such a way that, without regard for purely human counsel, they may devote themselves wholly to the work of the Gospel. This response cannot be given except with the inspiration and strength of the Holy Spirit."

DECREE ON THE CHURCH'S MISSIONARY ACTIVITY
(AD GENTES), 23–24

The impetus for Christian discernment is to understand God's will as best one can so as to decide the more generous response to God. It is to continue what began at our baptism when we were claimed for Christ and committed our lives to God. People discern in order to obtain clarity on how they best live out their baptismal commitment as they grow into adult Christians. This step assists the baptized Christian to intentionally seek one's life vocation according to God's plan. To discover the design that God has uniquely drawn for our life is part of the process of growing into a fully mature man or woman in Christ.

COMMITTING TO GOD'S DESIGN

SCRIPTURE: "Be doers of the word and not hearers only, deluding yourselves."

JAMES 1:22

REFLECTION: The great tragedy in contemporary life is that we are content to be good people, when we are called to greatness. Each one of us, after all, is called to be a saint. "Why so few saints?" one of my Dominican brothers mused. Is it simply that we don't want to do the work that saintliness calls for? Or that secretly we lack faith that it is even possible for someone like me to be a saint today. Saints are not perfect people. They are imperfect people constantly cooperating with God's grace in perfecting their minds, hearts and souls for their love of God and neighbor.

Saints are not people who have arrived; rather they are those women and men who faithfully journey with God. The secret to achieving sanctity is not to concentrate on the result (which is God's work), but to concentrate on the effort one makes day in and day out for God. To be a saint is to be committed and open to God's design instead of one's own. It is to daily walk the paths God beckons us to travel rather than following our own direction. Remember the words the angel Gabriel spoke to Mary: "...for nothing will be impossible for God" (Luke 1:37).

QUOTE: *"In my Word, I have already said everything. Fix your eyes on him alone, for in him I have revealed all and in him you will find more than you could ever ask for or desire."*

SAINT JOHN OF THE CROSS

ACTION: Stop and honestly ask yourself today if you truly believe that all things are possible with God. If you say, "yes," then consciously decide to live like it today in the choices you make.

PRAYER: Lord God, too often my gaze is on me instead of you. That's where I trip myself up. Deep down I want to be a saint, but it seems foolish and even presumptuous to say so knowing my questionable track record. Yet if I keep my eyes on you, I can trust you to take me where we both want me to go. Give me that strength this day.

LIVING IN THE PRESENT

SCRIPTURE: "Martha, Martha, you are anxious and worried about many things. There is need of only one thing. Mary has chosen the better part and it will not be taken from her."

LUKE 10:41–42

REFLECTION: So often, like Martha in the Gospel, the Lord challenges us to focus on the *unum necessarium*, the "one thing necessary." What is that one necessary thing next to which everything else pales and without which everything else is meaningless? It is a focused life lived in the presence of the Lord, moment by moment, task by task, encounter by encounter. Imagine what that would be like to go through our days with all their myriad activity and interactions, not simply as one separate person on our own, but as persons connected to the life of the Holy One.

My seminarian classmate Father John always says: "Live in the present with the Presence." Is this not at the heart of the gentle rebuke our Lord gives Martha? We human beings love to compartmentalize our lives into roles and responsibilities, but our Lord is saying, "Take me into all of it with you. I want to be there for you, sharing your ups and downs, your moments of frustration as well as of real joy and accomplishment."

The Lord is already there with us, of course, as he never leaves our side. It is we who leave the Lord in our conscious awareness and acknowledgement of God's presence. How strange to think that in a world so hungry for love and affirmation we don't daily tune in to the love and affirmation that is right there freely offered in every moment. So gently rebuke yourself whenever you step out of the awareness of the one who always stands in your presence, guiding, loving, and sharing each moment with you.

QUOTE: *"Be very patient and show in every way that you are servants of God. Say: And now, what I do I wait for? Is it not the Lord?"*
ORIGEN

ACTION: As you begin your day, let this be your mantra: "Today, I will stay in the present with the divine Presence." Center yourself back in the Lord whenever you catch yourself throughout this day absorbed with the past or worrying about the future.

God is with you always!

PRAYER: Loving Creator, give me the wisdom and strength to focus on the one thing necessary today: living in the present with you in all that I say, in all that I do, and in all those whom I meet this day.

DARE TO COMMIT

SCRIPTURE: "You will know the truth and the truth will set you free."

JOHN 8:32

REFLECTION: Why commit? As I sit here in the wave of summer heat and ponder commitment, a popular song by Ella Fitzgerald comes to mind. The song emphasizes that we should fall in love—now, and begs the question, why not? Fall in love, that is. This was one of my father's favorite songs, so I heard it frequently while growing up and it sounded convincing when I was young—yet now after a few more decades of life—the superficial thoughts jump out at me.

Falling in love—like committing oneself to a life choice—sounds light, easy, trite. Why shouldn't we commit? Now is the time for it. But I can't dismiss the song because it also has some strong thoughts about commitment—our hearts are made of it. Yet commitment to all walks of life and the steps that prepare us for lifelong fidelity are never easy.

Commitment is saying "yes" to the plan of God, and it may

mean saying "no" to dreams and nourished hopes for one's life. One person, one event, one word on a retreat can change the direction of a life and may lead us in a thousand different places. God "shows up" in so many unexpected faces, and his plan may be nothing that we could have asked for, imagined, or dreamed. Francis Thompson, in the book *Hound of Heaven,* speaks to my personal struggle by speaking of our tendency to run from God. We stop running when, like Mary, full of grace-filled awe, we find the courage to utter a "yes" from the unknown depths of our heart.

One statement that has brought me through thick and thin is that Jesus never said it would be easy. He did say, "I will be with you!"

–BY C.K.

QUOTE: *"God adorns the person chosen with all the gifts of the Spirit needed to fulfill the task at hand."*

SAINT BERNADINE OF SIENA

ACTION: Think of the people among your family and friends who are committed. Thank God for their example of commitment.

PRAYER: Lord Jesus, you know our hearts and our desire to please you in all that we do. Help us know the plan of life that you want us to follow.

HOLINESS

SCRIPTURE: "But, as he who calls you is holy, be holy yourselves in every aspect of your conduct."

1 PETER 1:15

REFLECTION: In The Dogmatic Constitution on the Church (*Lumen Gentium*), the universal call to holiness is clearly stated: "all Christians in whatever state or walk in life are called to the fullness of the Christian life and to the perfection of charity" (*LG* 40).

The Church is telling us that each Christian, whatever his or her state of life, is called to holiness. If I am a married woman, I am not to be holy in the way a cloistered nun is called to be. If I am a committed single person, I do not pursue my sanctity as a married couple would. The call to holiness is a call from God, thus it is God who desires our holiness. The Lord wills that we should be saved and also that we should become saints!

The word holiness implies a connection with the divine. The call to begin the journey toward holiness is quite simple. Whether it is getting out of bed in the morning, writing that long overdue letter, or the simple task of serving tea to the older neighbors, the greatest effort is taking that first step in the direction God calls you to go.

In order to share ever more fully in the unfathomable riches of Christ's own holiness, we must follow him faithfully. We are called to faithfulness—to spirituality and prayer in order to "stand up" to a culture that can be opposed to our life with God.

Perhaps a starting point will be to do everyday common tasks with an extraordinary love as Thérèse of Lisieux showed us. What price are we willing to pay to be messengers of holiness?

QUOTE: *"This daring ambition of aspiring to great sanctity has never left me. I don't rely on my own merits. I put all my confidence in him who is virtue and pure holiness."*

SAINT THÉRÈSE OF LISIEUX

ACTION: Ask in prayer for the grace, courage, and inspiration to commit to simple and ordinary deeds with extraordinary love!

PRAYER: O God, how I pray to act for you alone. May my life become a continual act of love that will one day bring me to the holiness that you, my God, want for me. I cannot do this alone; it is only with your help that I can be all that you have called me to be.

SURRENDER

SCRIPTURE: "Hear, O Israel! The LORD is our God, the LORD alone! Therefore, you shall love the LORD, your God, with your whole heart, and with your whole being, and with your whole strength. Take to heart these words which I command you today."

DEUTERONOMY 6:4–6

REFLECTION: Life is the adventure of learning to love and be loved. It's a process of discerning not only how to love, but what is worthy of my love. We can be attached to certain feelings and emotions along the way that paralyze us. But God does not call us to paralysis! For the saints, love is the horizon, not the boundary of human existence.

In other words, it is the expansive canvas upon which the large and small brushstrokes of our lives are painted in the choices of each day; it is the landscape against which we soar and flourish or settle into a safe mediocrity. The potential of our lives is utterly boundless and mirrors God's boundless love.

We often get hung up with the "whole heart, whole being, whole strength" part of the command. This instruction requires our total surrender to God's love. We wonder what will be left for ourselves, and a common fear is, "What if we lose ourselves in this?" Good question, and the reality is: You will!

God doesn't invite us to remain on the sidelines with the crowd, rather we are to enter the court of the cross. The cross, freely and trustingly embraced, sometimes feels like the brutal relinquishing of mind, heart, and strength to God's purposes. Still, as we begin to trust God, we will discover our surrender begins to feel like a dance. It is when we begin this dance that we realize that human hunger abandons itself into the out-stretched arms of divine longing because we can finally say to God: "not my will, but yours be done."

QUOTE: *"Look more deeply into the mirror and meditate on [Christ's] humility, what marvelous poverty....Ponder his unspeakable love which caused him to suffer on the wood of the cross and to endure the most shameful kind of death."*

SAINT CLARE OF ASSISI

ACTION: What are you being invited to let go of in your life today? What is God asking you to leave at the foot of the cross?

PRAYER: Lord of the dance, take my hands and lead me across the floor of life, holding me closer and closer to you as we make every move, every step, first here and then there. Turn and twist me to your direction, bending me ever so gently to your will and sweeping me across the tiles of time to our final pirouette.

FOLLOW CHRIST

SCRIPTURE: "I have the strength for everything through him who empowers me."

PHILIPPIANS 4:13

REFLECTION: One morning I was talking with a ninety-year-old priest from our community, Father Giles, and asked about his vocation. He shared his story about how in the 1930s he went to his pastor about entering the seminary. He was a farm boy from South Dakota and one of sixteen children. Supportive, the pastor wrote him a letter of recommendation. But he was rejected because he was not proficient in Latin.

Alfred Richard, known as Father Giles back then, loved to type and took as many typing classes as possible instead of studying language. He became, after a time, able to type ninety words per minute! Though Latin at that time was just a little more critical in the Church than typing. So at age nineteen, Alfred resolved to ride his horse five miles every day for a year—

come snow, rain or sleet—to his pastor, who tutored him in his Latin declensions. A year later he was accepted into seminary.

When I asked him how he made that disciplined commitment at his age, he said: "I don't know...I just did what I had to do. I simply did what it took to follow my calling...but the truth is, I didn't know then how I knew that!" Doing what one has to do, what it takes to follow one's calling without even being clear of the "why" or "how" is the essential task of a disciple of Christ; to step forward, as poet Kathleen Norris reflected, not on the outward authority of one's credentials for the mission but the inner authority of the call itself.

The powerful authority behind Jesus' words and works in the Gospel came not from his outward, earthly credentials. This poor, upstart preacher from Nazareth had none! Rather, it was Jesus' inner authority that gave an authentic and bold witness of love of God and neighbor. To do what it takes is an apt description of the disciplined, no-nonsense love Jesus commands of us in the Gospel, time and again. Gospel love does feel different than warm, fuzzy, comfortable notions of love. To be a disciple is to be disciplined. To be a disciple of Christ's is to exercise the discipline of love.

Love is the call, the journey, and the destination, rooted not first in any outward authority but in the inner authority of the one who calls: Jesus Christ our Lord.

QUOTE: *"The whole company of saints bears witness to the unfailing truth that, without real effort, no one wins the crown."*

SAINT THOMAS BECKET

ACTION: Do that one thing today that it takes to follow your vocation: Make the appointment, call the particular person, begin the book, or initiate the program that you have been putting off. In order to be accountable, tell a friend what that thing is for you.

PRAYER: Holy God, I think I need to have it all figured out before I act on something. I make ambiguity an enemy. Give me the courage to do what you ask of me with a loving, tenacious heart even when I don't understand fully your way.

WHAT MUST I DO?

SCRIPTURE: "Jesus, looking at him, loved him."

MARK 10:21

REFLECTION: When did you last listen and hear the movement of your heart? When did you look at your experience and discover that your heart was moving and seeking a new direction? When did you talk with a trusted friend or a wise mentor regarding choices that would impact your life decisions? Likely you will not be knocked off a horse like Paul in Damascus, see a vision like Mother Teresa in the streets of Calcutta, or hear a voice as Mary did in a cottage in Nazareth. God has sent you help to make difficult decisions and choices: But in order to discern these choices, you must listen in prayer, examine personal experience, and consult a trusted friend or friends.

In his book *He Leadeth Me*, Walter Ciszek, SJ, the American Jesuit who was detained in a Russian prison, experienced the many questions of a discerner when he was a young man. He was tormented by his obligations toward his family. He wondered about the many ways he could serve God and continually questioned his motives for serving God as a religious. He was fearful about the future and about making a commitment that was still filled with questions. How is one ever sure of the will of God? These types of questions became his nightmare.

All serious discerners will be able to identify with the questions in the heart of this holy man, Father Ciszek. All commitments in life involve moments of grace and doubt. There comes a moment when a decision must be made. God asks much because he knows how much each person has to give.

QUOTE: *"We are born to love, we live to love, and we will die to love still more."*

SAINT JOSEPH CAFASSO

ACTION: Let the Son of God fill you with his overwhelming love today! Let the questions in your heart rest in the heart of Christ.

PRAYER: My Jesus, my Savior, today I can identify with Mother Teresa as she looked at you and prayed with the words of Jesus: "I thirst!" If she had this struggle—then I, too, can ask for that same grace to respond to your call with faith, hope, and charity.

WHAT ON EARTH ARE YOU DOING FOR HEAVEN'S SAKE?

SCRIPTURE: "He has bestowed on us the precious and very great promises, so that through them you may come to share in the divine nature."

2 PETER 1:4

REFLECTION: The parish priest's booming voice resounded during a parish mission: "What on earth are you doing for heaven's sake?" From that day on, Father's homily had everyone in the Kiley household talking about heaven. So what is this mystery place called heaven, the family asked? In his inimitable style, Dad Kiley's response to wide eyes and curious looks was: "Heaven is the place where we are all going to live with God some day."

Casey remembered her question—is it a place to see, to visit, or to stay? Since this household experienced life in the Catholic world of Baltimore Catechism 101, no further questions were invited. However, it was a question that resounded in Casey's heart for years to come. It marked the first time in her young life when she briefly thought about the future. In later years it became: What am I doing with my life for heaven's sake?

Trying to live for heaven was a source of strength and challenge. The seeds of a call to religious life began early. In teenage years, fights with God included: "No, not me! Why me? Maybe me?" Excuses such as Jeremiah's "I am too young" (Jeremiah 1:7) and Moses' "I am slow of speech and tongue" (Exodus 4:10) became mantras of Casey's journey. This theme of living for heaven is a life call.

Casey's fear is not wrong but very human. We all feel inadequate to the task, but we need to remember that God knows us better than we know ourselves. Recall the words that the Lord spoke to Jeremiah the prophet, "Before I formed you in the womb I knew you, before you were born I dedicated you, a prophet to the nations I appointed you....Do not say, 'I am too young.' To whomever I send you, you shall go; whatever I command you, you shall speak. Do not be afraid of them, for I am with you to deliver you—oracle of the LORD" (Jeremiah 1:5, 7–8).

QUOTE: *"If we seek God, God will appear to us: and if we hold God, God will stay with us."*

SAINT ARSENIUS

ACTION: Pray the Our Father slowly with thoughts of eternal life—"as it is in heaven."

PRAYER: Good and gracious God, I am awed at the wonders and the mysteries of life that surround me. I am inspired to respond to all that you ask of me.

GOD PERFECTS ME

SCRIPTURE: "May the God of peace make you perfect in holiness. May he preserve you whole and entire, spirit, soul, and body, irreproachable at the coming of our Lord Jesus Christ. He who calls us is trustworthy, therefore he will do it."

1 THESSALONIANS 5:23–24

REFLECTION: Sanctity is a universal call. We are all called to holiness by virtue of our baptism: our entrance into the Church, the body of Christ, and the very life of God's friendship results from our baptism. The initial spark of holiness that took place at our baptism was strengthened through the gift of confirmation, when the gifts of the Holy Spirit are lavishly poured upon our souls as at Pentecost. In that biblical event, the first Christians were given the courage needed to boldly and unapologetically bear witness to Christ. And they did, often with their very lives.

We are called to the same radical witness. This witness becomes possible when we grow into a holiness not based on our pursuit of perfectionism, but on God's perfecting work within us. Of ourselves we can do nothing, but with Christ we can do everything, Saint Paul reminds us. What we strive for in daily holiness, then, is a constancy of purpose and effort based not on what we can do, but what God can do in us. He who calls us is trustworthy, therefore he will do it.

QUOTE: *"Under the impulse of love, which the Holy Spirit pours into their hearts (see Romans 5:5), they live more and more for Christ and his body, the Church (see Colossians 1:24). The more fervently therefore they join themselves to Christ by this gift of their entire life, the fuller does the Church's life become and the more vigorous and fruitful its apostolate."*

Perfectae Caritatis, 1

ACTION: Stop and reflect midday on where your attention is focused. Is it on yourself and your own frustrated attempts at perfectionism or on God, allowing his grace free reign to perfect you from within?

PRAYER: Faithful friend, when I try to run my own life, remind me that is your job, not mine. Allow me to give myself permission today to love my imperfect self as it is while remaining open to your perfecting work of grace within.

PART III

How Does a Person Begin Discerning?
The Elements of Discernment

"Whether you are married, in the generous single life, priesthood, or religious life, do not be afraid. The foundation of a vocation is the same: the call to love."

THE MOST REVEREND EDWARD M. RICE
AUXILIARY BISHOP OF ST. LOUIS

We begin discerning right in the garden of our own "particular moment in history." The actual "stuff" of discernment is taken from the events, encounters, and efforts of our everyday lives. What are our life experiences?

It is necessary to ask questions: What is the pattern of divine love in my life? How does God continually relate to me and call me into relationship? What has God planted in the soil of my personality? What are some clues to how the gifts, talents, and desires God has granted continue to surface and blossom in my life? These are the seeds of my vocation that the Lord is bringing to full flower within me. As Saint Thomas observes, our nature is the foundation upon which God graces us. God is not looking for you to offer a different self, but your truest self.

GOD WILL GRANT YOUR HEART'S DESIRE

SCRIPTURE: "Find your delight in the LORD who will give you your heart's desire."

PSALM 37:4

REFLECTION: I don't think I'm being paranoid, but I think I'm being followed. Lately, no matter what priory or rectory or hotel I stay in around the country, the same commercial comes on the television for some restaurant I've never heard of called The Golden Corral. Yes, I'm being followed by a commercial! After an appetizing, sumptuous spread of mouthwatering foods, it's seductive, and this sound bite suggests, help yourself to happiness.

The commercial's tag line, "Help yourself to happiness," could be Jesus' billboard slogan for Christian discipleship. At first glance, what Jesus serves up to his disciples (poverty, hunger, grief, and hatred) do not strike one as appetizing or alluring. Nor does what Jesus asks of us strike one as the most effective vocation pitch: *Come be poor and hungry with me.... The experience will make you weep, and by the way, be sure that hanging out with me will leave you excluded and insulted.*

Yet Jesus summons us to radically reorder our priorities and our way of seeing the world. It's a summons to reexamine and redirect our pursuit of happiness not in pursuit of something, but *Someone*!

How are you finding your direction? In what way are you discerning God's will at this moment of your life? And toward whom are you turning? The answer to this question is critical, as it will help you discover true happiness, based on God's promise to accompany and be with us always. Here we can acknowledge that it is not one's circumstances that we should worry about but our response to them. If our response is to pursue the trust and hope of God's strength, rather than our own, we will know the sustaining joy and delight that form the foundation of every authentic Christian vocation.

QUOTE: *"If charity, as Saint Paul says, means to weep with those who weep and to rejoice with those who are glad, then, dearest mother, you shall rejoice exceedingly that God, in his grace and his love for you, is showing me the path to true happiness, and assuring me that I shall never lose him."*

SAINT ALOYSIUS GONZAGA

ACTION: Examine through quiet prayer all the ways you have sought out happiness up to this point in your life. Honestly ask yourself in what direction your pursuit for happiness is taking you today. Are you turned firmly toward God or subtly away from God? Write a letter to God to complete your examination.

PRAYER: Loving Father, you have given me so much! Be patient with my foolish resistance at times to trust you fully. With your grace, guide my discernment through the many voices that seek my attention, and help me to know the false from the true. Most of all, let me not be distracted from my ultimate goal: finding my happiness in you!

MARITAL LOVE MIRRORS CHRIST'S LOVE

SCRIPTURE: "Whatever is true, whatever is honorable, whatever is just, whatever is pure, whatever is lovely, whatever is gracious, if there is any excellence and if there is anything worthy of praise, think about these things."

PHILIPPIANS 4:8

REFLECTION: In its 2009 pastoral letter, "Marriage: Love and Life in the Divine Plan," the United States Conference of Catholic Bishops writes that "a marriage upon which (Christ's) school of gratitude and openness has left its mark of joy and warmth is a sign of the kingdom."

At the heart of every vocation is foundational gratitude for the gift of God's call and the openness to deepen it, not simply for one's own spiritual good but for the spiritual value provided to others edified by its witness. That witness is most apparent when joy, warmth, gratitude, and openness radiate from our lives as we follow Christ.

Unfortunately, many people do not think of marriage as a vocation that is meant to be a sign of the kingdom of God in our midst in the same way as they might for the priesthood and religious life. In fact, according to the Center for Applied Research in the Apostolate, a recent survey revealed that out of Catholics ranging in age from twenty-six to forty-six, only twenty-four percent believe marriage is a vocation.

Yet, again and again the Church reminds the faithful that marriage is an authentic calling from God. It's the primary pathway to holiness whereby two travel the road together toward heaven, gratefully bearing the fruit and responsibility of children along the way. Marital love mirrors the profound love Christ has for his Church.

QUOTE: *"Authentic married love is caught up in divine love and is directed and enriched by the redemptive power of Christ and the salvific action of the Church, with the result that the spouses are effectively led to God and helped and strengthened in their lofty roles as fathers and mothers."*

PASTORAL CONSTITUTION ON THE
CHURCH IN THE MODERN WORLD (*GAUDIUM ET SPES*), 48

ACTION: As you consider how God is calling you, think about the people who have been a sign of God's love in your life. Do you think of marriage as a pathway to holiness? Perhaps there is a couple in your life that models Christ's love in the gift of holy matrimony. Take the time to reflect and write down your thoughts on how a man and woman bring each other closer to Christ through marriage.

PRAYER: Lord of love and fidelity, we know that when two people come together in faith and create an "us," you are the center of that bond. Help us grow in gratitude for the gift of the other whereby we see and hear and touch your presence in the one you have given me to love.

BRINGING PEOPLE TO CHRIST

SCRIPTURE: "So also faith of itself, if it does not have works, is dead."

JAMES 2:17

REFLECTION: When I was in the eighth grade, I remember sitting on the top stair of our two-story home one afternoon after school with my big brother, Larry. He was patient with my premature anxieties about not knowing what I wanted to be when I grew up. Not long into our conversation, he asked me point blank: "Well, what's the most important thing to you in life?"

I answered without hesitation, "Bringing people to Christ."

Then my brother said, "You must follow that wherever it takes you."

Since I am named after the Apostle Andrew, it is striking to me how this has dovetailed so neatly with my vocation. This is not only true as a religious but also within my ministry as a vocation director. The impetus of Christian vocation is not just to make Jesus the priority of my life for me, but to share his mission of gathering all unto the Creator, an ongoing apostolate of outreach to and for others' salvation. The Church is, after all, apostolic, which is recited in our Creed every Sunday at Mass; and Twelve Apostles stand as models of those who came to understand these tenets of faith.

As Saint John suggests in his Gospel, in the same breath that Saint Andrew was saying "Yes, Lord, I'll follow you, where do you live?" he was witnessing to someone else: "You have to meet this guy! He's the one we've been waiting for."

Andrew was immediately eager to bring others to Christ, and the most well-known example of this was his brother, Simon, who was named Peter. Andrew was joyfully surprised in meeting Jesus. He was determined not to keep this treasure to himself but to spend a lifetime bringing it to others. Andrew recognized Christ as the true desire for whom their hearts were longing and waiting to meet!

QUOTE: *"Finally, if you truly want to help the soul of your neighbor, you should approach God first with all your heart. Ask him simply to fill you with charity, the greatest of these virtues; with it you can accomplish what you desire."*

SAINT VINCENT FERRER

ACTION: Faith is meant to be shared. It comes alive when it is shared. Speak to two people today explicitly about your friendship with Christ. Then reflect on the experience of speaking openly and vulnerably about your own encounter with Jesus.

PRAYER: Christ Jesus, all of my hope is in your friendship. Help me to bring that hope alive by speaking it out loud to others.

PAY IT FORWARD

SCRIPTURE: "Seek out the LORD and his might; constantly seek his face."

PSALM 105:4

REFLECTION: In discernment readings, Saint Ignatius of Loyola suggests that we imagine ourselves at the end of our lives. The question Ignatius recommends we ask is, when faced with death, what pieces of our lives are we happy to remember?

When asked to write the introduction for a jubilee celebration, this question from the Spiritual Exercises came to mind. I reflected on the dedication for my fellow religious:

"For fifty years of religious profession, you have proclaimed that Jesus Christ has been the center, the source, and the treasure of your life! How wonderfully appropriate that today, the feast of Pentecost, we are called to depend on the inspiration and light of the Holy Spirit in our mission of making the heart of Christ known and loved! To follow Jesus as a religious has indeed been a humbling honor—to think that our Lord chose you for himself! With hearts of deep gratitude, we thank God for the witness, example, and dedication manifested in your life. You have been a true apostle, chosen by God, who recognized the love of God poured into your heart. You entered into a covenant with God through professing vows of poverty, chastity, and obedience. We applaud your commitment, and we celebrate your years of service to the people in your care. We have been blessed to have you among us. May you continue to be blessed as you have given—without measure. May the Spirit of God be with you as you walk the path toward his loving embrace."

What will be said of each of us after fifty years (or more) of fidelity? How often do we take a sneak peek of our future?

Fast-forward fifty years and reflect on your ending. What do you want God to bring into fruition in your life? How will you choose to be faithful to your commitments?

QUOTE: *"Choose now what you would wish to have chosen at life's end."*

SAINT ANTHONY MARY CLARET

ACTION: Journal about the many graces of your life and write your own eulogy.

PRAYER: Dear Jesus, help me to live each day knowing that at the end of the day—in the evening of life—we shall be judged only on love.

IS GOD ENOUGH?

SCRIPTURE: "A light from the sky suddenly flashed around him. He fell to the ground and heard a voice saying to him..."I am Jesus...." ACTS 9:3–5

REFLECTION: Is God enough? In the midst of Vince's successful Yale law experience, the chaplain posed a question that opened up an unexpected journey within his heart. With all that you have and are, with all that you have waiting for you after graduation, can God be enough for you? Completely taken off-guard by the question, Vince began an intense soul-searching journey to test the question. Was it a life question that he had been avoiding?

How can this be—my life is mapped out for me...a great future full of hope in a world of need! thought Vince. There are many people to serve, and Vince was known to be other-centered and justice-driven. His life direction had been planned for years in his heart and mind. Yet, as God broke in on his agenda, the thought that the Lord was asking him this question was haunting.

When one is invited to a life of discipleship, Christ will map out the journey and the conditions involved: sacrificial giving, lifelong service to others, and a participation in suffering for the sake of others. The hundredfold is promised to those who give all in this life, and Christ has prepared an eternal banquet for all the faithful.

What do you think? Is God enough?

QUOTE: *"Lord...give me only your love and your grace. That is enough for me."*

SAINT IGNATIUS OF LOYOLA

ACTION: Consider the thoughts of the spiritual masters who have gone before us. Live calmly and quietly today in pure faith. Do not let yourself worry about the questions swirling around in your heart and mind.

PRAYER: From the abundance of my heart I entrust this gift of self into your welcoming arms, O Christ. In this walk of faith I pray to be able to experience joy as I share my faith with others.

GOT PASSION?

SCRIPTURE: "...Stir into flame the gift of God that you have...."
2 Timothy 1:6

REFLECTION: Glancing at the end-of-the-year news, one message stands out: What the world and our Church need are people who are filled with the fire and passion to lay down their lives for Christ! At a recent national conference for Catholic Bishops, the Most Reverend Timothy M. Dolan, Archbishop of New York, said: "Love for Jesus and his Church must be the passion of our lives!" (USCCB, November 2011 General Assembly presidential address.)

We are called to live with holy zeal, not just toy with the notion of it. To do this, we can regard the passion of the first apostles and the life of Christ as he walked among the people in the Gospels. We recall with awe the fervor of our mentors and models in community, ministry, parishes, classrooms, and offices. We prayerfully ponder the zeal of Saint Teresa of Ávila, Saint Francis Xavier, Saint Catherine of Siena, and all of the saints. Thinking about being zealous is easier than actually living it out with a burning fire! Zeal was not a passing thought to any of these individuals.

What would nurture in me the inner strength to give without counting the cost? We cannot ignite the fire of love and revitalize the dormant areas by ourselves. We need each other, and we need Jesus Christ. Our God is a consuming fire. Can we live with passion and evangelize our culture?

QUOTE: *"Happy the man who knows how to control zeal. Let your zeal be inflamed with charity, adorned with knowledge, and established in constancy. True zeal is the child of charity, since it is its ardor. Therefore, like charity, it is patient and kind. It is without quarreling, without hatred, without envy; it rejoices in the truth."*

SAINT FRANCIS DE SALES

ACTION: Reflect on the mentors in your life who bring light and joy and inspire you to be a bearer of God's love and a healer in the lives of others.

PRAYER: We pray with the saints devoted to your Sacred Heart. Come, heart of Jesus, and give us your heart that we may spread the love of your heart with a renewed fire. Set a flame in my heart that will be strong and enkindle new love in our world.

PUT ON CHRIST

SCRIPTURE: "Put on the Lord Jesus Christ."

ROMANS 13:14

REFLECTION: A few weeks ago, my fellow sisters and I heard a homily where the preacher was reflecting on the reading from Saint Paul: "Clothe yourselves—'put on the Lord Jesus Christ'" (Romans 13:14). The homilist recounted an experience of driving through a city neighborhood as the people from the church were congregating following Sunday services.

Each parishioner emerged from the church dressed in Sunday finery, which one might know as "dressed to the nines" or one's "Sunday best." The question was posed: "Wouldn't it be great if we would all clothe ourselves in love as some people clothe themselves for important events?" This is not a simple task. It is indeed a great challenge for Christians to embrace: "Put on then, as God's chosen ones, holy and beloved, heartfelt compassion, kindness, humility, gentleness, and patience" (Colossians 3:12).

Some questions that might emerge from Saint Paul's mandate include:

1. How has God revealed to me a sacred call to be clothed in love?
2. What has God accomplished in me that has revealed to me how chosen I am?
3. How might I be challenged to be clothed in compassion and forgiveness?

QUOTE: *"Bring to everyone a ray of that holy tenderness of the heart of Jesus."*

MOTHER CLELIA MERLONI
SERVANT OF GOD

ACTION: Ponder the following: What call to action do the above Scripture passages evoke in me? How do these passages affect and alter my spiritual life? Is God asking more of me?

PRAYER: Let us pray that we may be clothed with love, which binds everything together in perfect harmony. May the peace of Christ rule in our hearts.

A UNIQUE MISSION

SCRIPTURE: "Conduct yourselves as worthy of the God who calls you into his kingdom and glory."

1 THESSALONIANS 2:12

REFLECTION: When I was a young boy, I awoke one day with my ear so swollen I could not get a knit cap around it as I got ready for school. I was rushed to the hospital and was operated on that day. The doctors told me that a common ear infection had gotten out of control, spread dangerously, and almost cost me my life in surgery that very day.

A month later, I went into surgery and again was almost lost on the operating table. When I asked my mother how one cheats death twice, she answered: "I don't really know. What I do know is that God must have a special mission for you; something he wants you to do that only you can do."

Those simple but faith-filled words were a profound catalyst as I began my search for a life vocation. What was God's mission and plan? And how could I be sure not to miss it? Likely this is a question that most of us ask at some point or another. We are called to give our lives away, and each person is a steward entrusted with a mission. Discovering our mission and being faithful to it is our life's task, the very meaning our lives.

QUOTE: *"If you ask how such things can occur, seek the answer in God's grace, not in doctrine; in the sighs of prayer, not in research; seek the bridegroom, not the teacher; God and not man; darkness,*

not daylight; and look not to the light but rather to the raging fire
that carries the soul to God with intense fervor and glowing fire."

SAINT BONAVENTURE

ACTION: What is the catalyst for your search for your life's mission? Embrace the opportunity today to rediscover that catalyst by meditating upon its source and meaning.

PRAYER: Divine Mentor, you have given me some work in this life that you have not given to another. Help me to listen today to the promptings of the Holy Spirit, guiding me to the mission that is mine in this moment, in this encounter, in this task, and in these circumstances of my life.

RUN TO WIN

SCRIPTURE: "LORD, my allotted portion and my cup, you have made my destiny secure. Pleasant places were measured out for me; fair to me indeed is my inheritance."

PSALM 16:5–6

REFLECTION: Discernment is like a marathon. How we prepare for it makes all the difference if we don't want to run aimlessly but instead achieve our goal, which is God's will as we best discern it at this moment. Some of life's miles are light and easy while others are arduous beyond measure. We have peaks and valleys in our effort to endure the long-distance run of discernment. But if we are sincerely discerning his plan for our lives, we can be confident that God is with us at each benchmark, running right alongside us, and cheering us on. This spirit can be likened to a gregarious wall of well-wishers, much like those we witness at any marathon. God will enthusiastically encourage us, but he cannot run the race for us. The Lord wants us to freely own the prize with confidence and peace. Without our effort and investment, there is no free or true ownership.

Seasons of discernment, then, are periods we need for amplified strength training to recognize and freely choose the next step God calls us to in our spiritual lives. To exercise the muscles of faith, hope, and love, we need some "workout equipment" provided by the Church. Some examples include: staying close to the sacraments of Eucharist and reconciliation, daily personal prayer and spiritual reading, spiritual direction, personal devotions such as Eucharistic Adoration or reciting the Chaplet of Divine Mercy, a network of supportive friends rooted in faith, *Come & See Vocation Weekends*, and follow-up visits to religious houses or rectories to experience the day-to-day lives of religious and priests while discerning particular religious calls.

When exploring the vocation of the single life or marriage, you would connect with retreat opportunities or workshops that would provide insight into these vocations. These various "exercises of discernment" discipline our spiritual selves and move us step-by-step toward the finish line, the imperishable prize of God's will being uniquely accomplished in us!

QUOTE: *"All with eyes to see can discover in it a complete gymnasium for the soul, a stadium for all the virtues, equipped for every kind of exercise; it is for each to choose the kind he [or she] judges best to gain the prize."*

SAINT AMBROSE

ACTION: Regarding your specific discernment, concretely practice an act for each of the theological virtues today: faith, hope, and love. Share with a friend the three actions and how they enriched your life.

PRAYER: Divine coach, let the growing desire to truly know and do your will ever more clearly and faithfully in my life motivate me to take action in my discernment efforts.

FINDING THE BEST WAY

SCRIPTURE: "As the Father loves me so I also love you. Remain in my love. If you keep my commandments, you will remain in my love, just as I have kept my Father's commandments and remain in his love."

JOHN 15:9–10

REFLECTION: A twenty-two-year-old man recently came to see me wondering about a possible religious vocation. After listening to him for some time, I challenged him, "Why are you so sure you have a religious vocation? Why are you so intent that you are supposed to live it out as a priest?" He replied without hesitation, "Because it is the best way for me to fully love God. And what do we really have at the end of our lives,

Father Wisdom, but our love for God and God's love for us?"

Indeed, what do we have? When all is said and done, all we have is our relationship with God, which becomes real as we live out the commandments to love God and our neighbor. As Saint John of the Cross writes: "In the evening of life, we will be judged by our love." If the whole point of our lives is to love as God loves, then we must find the best way. So what path, what road might God be revealing to you? Take the first step along that road.

QUOTE: *"Late have I loved you, O Beauty ever ancient, ever new, late have I loved you! You were within me, but I was outside, and it was there that I searched for you. In my unloveliness I plunged into the lovely things which you created. You were with me but I was not with you."*

SAINT AUGUSTINE

ACTION: In the end, our life is a summary of yesterday's choices. Reflect on recent missed opportunities to love God and neighbor. Resolve on seizing those unlimited chances God gives you today for the best way to love as he has loved. Often enough, simply "wasting time" with another is the most generous gesture of love. Generously "waste" some time today with God and the unexpected "neighbor" he sends your way.

PRAYER: Lord, help me not to take for granted the constant, faithful love you show me in the events and encounters of each day, but to be a radiant reflection of that love to all I meet. In all I say and do, may I mirror *you* today. For the more intentionally I love you and my neighbor, the closer I draw to my vocation.

TRANSFORM THE WORLD

SCRIPTURE: "So we are ambassadors for Christ, as if God were appealing through us. We implore you on behalf of Christ, be reconciled to God."

2 CORINTHIANS 5:20

REFLECTION: We are all called to transform the secular world around us for, in, and through Christ. This is not just a ministry for the religious or those ordained but for those who are married and single as well. While marriage is the most common vocation lived out in God's people, its commonality does not render it any less beautiful or compelling. Marriage is a sacred context for the ongoing work of the kingdom.

This is why Jesus had little patience with the legalistic approach to marriage in his time when divorce was so common. The husband could divorce his wife over something as simple as a bad meal. Jesus elevates marriage from a contractual agreement to a sacramental one. He approaches marriage as a vocation, a spiritual path that two people embark upon not solely for themselves, but as a channel of grace that helps both become another Christ for the world. Through the commitment a husband and wife make to one another, they mirror Christ's passionate love for his Church. The witness of that faithful, spousal love reflects the depth of God's faithful love for humanity and the living continuation of his mission to reconcile all people to himself.

QUOTE: *[The relationship between God and the soul] "is like the experience of two persons here on earth who love each other deeply and understand each other well; even without signs, just by a glance, it seems, they understand each other. Those two lovers gaze directly at each other."*

SAINT TERESA OF ÁVILA

ACTION: Make an appointment with yourself for a period of spiritual reading one evening on the sacramental nature and purpose of marriage. Look online to find some of Blessed John Paul II's writings on the subject.

PRAYER: Faithful God, my deepest desire is to do your will in all that I do. Free me from all selfish interest as I discern your plan for my life. If you are calling me to marriage, help me not to look merely for what I can get out of it for myself. Rather, help me enter into the life of another and through him or her help me to see you.

JOYFUL PRESENCE

SCRIPTURE: "I proclaim to you good news of great joy!"

LUKE 2:10

REFLECTION: To be a Christian who will evangelize others, we need to be joyful and tell the world by our expression what great things God has done for us. The angel said to Mary: "Hail, favored one! The Lord is with you" (Luke 1:28), which in some translations is recorded as "rejoice, highly favored one." When we are aware that we are favored in God's eyes, we will attract others to Christ through our spirit of joyful presence.

We may never know the many lives we have touched or will touch by the joy reflected in our words, a simple smile, or through our daily routines. Once, I received a letter twenty years after a student had left my class. She wanted me to know how much the class had helped her learn to accept herself and laugh at the little foibles of life that make us smile. She was able to transfer the lighthearted spirit to her college dorm and to a workplace in the corporate world. People complimented her on her ability to transform the workplace from a negative place to a place of relaxation, comfort, and enthusiasm. Everyone enjoys an office or a laboratory that has a sense of purpose yet is able to maintain the light spirit of cheerful balance. Knowing that I had somehow contributed to the joy of this young lady delighted me greatly.

Pope John XXIII was known for his great sense of humor; he did not allow the weight of his office to affect his amiable relationship with everyone in the Vatican. When asked how many people work in the Vatican, he said with a slight grin, "About half of them!" Into every life a little rain must fall, but the sunshine coming through is not to be taken lightly. It is a sign of the presence of God shining upon the world.

–BY C.K.

QUOTE: *"Christian joy is a gift from God flowing from a good conscience."*

SAINT PHILLIP NERI

ACTION: Recall the people in your life today who reflect *joyful* living. Thank God for them in prayer and tell them how much they mean to you, reminding them of God's love for them.

PRAYER: Lord, help me to keep some parts of the day in balance. Let me see light in the people and events that can be lifted up!

PART IV

Does Discernment Lead to Action?

"God gave us free will; the free will to decide. The fruit of discernment is decision."

CARL WISDOM, MARRIED LAYMAN

"A decision like this demands a certain struggle. It cannot be otherwise. But then [comes] the certainty; this is the right thing! Yes, the Lord wants me, and he will give me strength. If I listen to him and walk with him, I become truly myself. What counts is not the fulfillment of my desires, but of his will."

POPE BENEDICT XVI
MESSAGE OF HIS HOLINESS FOR THE
TWENTY-SIXTH WORLD YOUTH DAY, AUGUST 6, 2010

Discernment is both an interior and an exterior exercise. Interiorly we pray daily about why, what, and how we are discerning. We read quietly and prayerfully those books and articles that aid our discernment, listening for God to speak through them. We make time daily to sit still and silently before God.

Exteriorly, we talk to those who live out the various vocational choices: married people, those who have chosen to be single for Christ, priests, and religious. We seek spiritual direction and offer a daily examination of conscience. Here we make time for vocational discernment on weekends and follow-up visits to those who are living out the call.

We are honest about our questions, fears, doubts, and concerns. Then, at some point, after interior prayer and exterior exploration, we make the best decision possible, knowing that faith is not certainty but the assurance of things hoped for. Finally, we ask God to open our hearts so that we may see the next step.

FORGETTING OURSELVES ON PURPOSE

SCRIPTURE: "Have among yourselves the same attitude that is also yours in Christ Jesus, Who though he was in the form of God, did not regard equality with God something to be grasped. Rather, he emptied himself, taking the form of a slave, coming in human likeness...."

PHILIPPIANS 2:5–7

REFLECTION: Recently, a friend announced with great fanfare, "Father, I have a gift for you." I received and opened it gratefully. Big, bold, typeset letters on a severe, forest-green book sleeve greeted me: *Forgetting Ourselves on Purpose.*

This book aptly describes the calling of all baptized Christians, as well as the holy ambition behind all Christian vocations. Forgetting ourselves and making a conscious decision to do so demands a love that faith makes known to us. In these moments, we freely choose to die purposefully to ourselves and to the attachment to our own will. Our voices often insist and subtly suggest to us: I am my own! Our lives, in fact, only have meaning in the constant, purposeful self-surrender to the love that invites us to continually open our hearts and allow Christ to fill, speak, and live within us.

The book's subtitle further described the text I received as: *Vocation and the Ethics of Ambition.* When we live our lives out of a sense of vocation, we are ambitious for the right things in life, such as knowing the Lord. We risk stepping out of the safety of the crowd, beyond the smallness of our own goals to encounter Jesus. When we truly understand that our first and most fundamental call is to be a follower of Jesus, we will take immediate action to change our life. This change is always simultaneously a risk and an invitation to encounter Christ authentically.

QUOTE: *"And when you have done these things, my eyes will be upon you and my ears attentive to your prayers; and before you call upon my name I shall say to you: Behold, I am here. What could be more delightful...than the voice of our Lord's invitation to us?"*
SAINT BENEDICT

ACTION: Practice forgetting yourself on purpose today. Hint: Notice how many times you use "I" in a conversation.

PRAYER: Jesus, I know following you will cost me my own agenda and plans, easy popularity, my own preoccupations, even my fears and wants that I am so attached to. But that price is nothing compared to the reward of your intimate friendship in which we discover that nothing needs to be proved, earned, or possessed. Only savored.

READY FOR THE PLUNGE

SCRIPTURE: "Come to me, all you who labor and are burdened, and I will give you rest."

MATTHEW 11:28

REFLECTION: As we prepare for transitions, many thoughts scramble around inside of us. Each transition takes a leap of faith of sorts, even if the people we meet as we transition are accommodating and welcoming. In these moments, the heart prepares to change, to break open and let a little more light in. Moments of transition teach us and assist us to begin to see the God who is always there.

One of the goals of formation is to grow in maturity and self-knowledge. Words from a young discerner capture some of these sentiments: "Suddenly looking around and seeing that my friends weren't there, my family wasn't there, heck, my car wasn't even there, I knew instantly what I had come for."

Sometimes God takes you to unexpected lands to speak to your heart. Christ asks you to shed your security blanket and gingerly step onto God's magic-carpet ride. In the beginning, this can be a wonderful time to immerse you in the culture of religious life while simply discerning and exploring your innermost questions. Some questions that you might ask include: God, will you please give me clarity in my call? Am I called to be religious? Am I called to be here, in this place, now? Where and how are you calling me? Help me to be open to your divine will in my life.

While these questions are important, God will continue to probe us with deeper questions. Are we willing to trust God with our most heartfelt and difficult questions? Are we willing to let go and take a ride—one that could prove to be the best ride of our life? Are we willing to go to this point or do we protest and say, "Don't ask me that, God!"

As soon as one starts letting go, little by little answers become clearer—an increase of peace, a sense of purpose, a growing self-confidence. These things may seem small, but they are truly gifts. As long as we continue to live a life in God, what do we have to fear?

QUOTE: *The interior life is like a sea of love in which the soul is plunged and is, as it were, drowned in love.*

SAINT JOHN VIANNEY

ACTION: Try to accept the challenges of today with a lighthearted spirit, knowing that God's plan is moving you forward.

PRAYER: Loving God, we pray with hope and expectation. We thank you for the grace of new beginnings and new possibilities.

"WASTING TIME" WITH GOD

SCRIPTURE: "Rejoice in the Lord, always. I shall say it again: rejoice! Your kindness should be known to all. The Lord is near. Have no anxiety at all, but in everything, by prayer and petition, with thanksgiving, make your requests known to God. Then the peace of God that surpasses all understanding will guard your hearts and minds in Christ Jesus."

PHILIPPIANS 4:4–7

REFLECTION: The story is told of an eleven-year-old boy who overheard his parents talking about contemplative prayer. He popped into the room and asked, "Mommy and Daddy, is that like when the outside noises get smaller and the inside noises get louder?"

An ancient definition of prayer is "to keep company with God." This approach goes beyond the traditional notion of prayer as something that we say or do. It suggests prayer is more a stance we take in life, an attitude of attentive awareness to the presence of God in whom "we live and move and have our being" (Acts 17:28). Far from being a static ritual or a mere rote recitation of words, prayer is being with someone and a recognition of his constant presence.

Prayer progresses ideally from verbal, to meditative (image-filled), and emerges eventually into the contemplative (image-less) whereby we sit in silence before God. In a contemplative state, we begin to silence our thoughts and find rest in the Lord. Silence is God's language and requires of us a posture of deep and peaceful listening. It is not a time to be productive, but an opportunity to "waste time" with God. When we truly love people, we "waste time" with them. It is the same with God.

QUOTE: *"If a [person] wants to be always in God's company, [he or she] must pray regularly and read regularly. When we pray, we talk to God. When we read, God talks to us. All spiritual growth comes from reading and reflection."*

SAINT ISIDORE

ACTION: Today as you go about your many roles and responsibilities, keep company with God. Whatever you are doing, try to stay present to the companion who never wants to leave your company.

PRAYER: Loving God, why do I always think I have to be productive to be worth something? Living in the shadow of your constant company is enough. I am at home wherever I am.

LISTEN WITH YOUR HEART

SCRIPTURE: "And your ears shall hear a word behind you: 'This is the way; walk in it,' when you would turn to the right or the left."

ISAIAH 30:21

REFLECTION: Hearing-aid owners know the radical change in their lives when they actually own up to the fact that they need an aid and finally purchase one to wear daily. The benefit is not only hearing what they were missing before but being fully engaged in conversations and interacting with life in a way that was not possible before. When you don't hear well, you don't participate as well or as frequently.

So often the words Jesus speaks in the Gospel jar our acoustics the way a good hearing aid radically alters the quality and clarity of our hearing. How attuned is our spiritual ear to the familiar call of Jesus: "Follow me?"

In the Scriptures, we see there are degrees, levels, and a gradual depth of giving oneself over to follow Christ. We are perhaps the zealous scribe who speaks earnestly (but a bit naïvely) of following Jesus wherever he goes. Or can we identify with the disciple who had just one other important thing to take care of first before following completely?

Yet Jesus' words are clear. "Follow me! Know what you are getting into, but do not be afraid to choose me now in this moment. Close the back doors, all the little escape hatches and come. It is true that some of these roads may seem difficult, and others you may rather avoid."

But will you allow Christ to lead you today?

As we shift our ability to hear, listening for Christ's voice, we will notice a major shift in our living. The Word of God is our hearing aid, tuning us in to full engagement with the charismatic carpenter of Nazareth, Jesus our Lord. It's much easier to pull back and be half-present than to risk full engagement. When we begin to recognize who represents our deepest need, live the Gospel call to follow Jesus, and embrace the call to holiness daily, we will come to know a radical new change in our lives because our relationship with God will transform and shape our lives.

QUOTE: *"Open up your ears. Enjoy the fragrance of eternal life, breathed on you by means of the sacraments."*

SAINT AMBROSE

ACTION: Identify two things the Word of God is calling you to act on...and then act on them this day!

PRAYER: Lord Jesus, truth be told, I like to talk more than listen. But then how will I hear you as the inspirations of the Holy Spirit speak to me each day if I don't tune in to your voice? Discipline my listening, Lord, so that I might fully engage in the conversation you want to have with me, heart to heart.

OPEN THE DOOR

SCRIPTURE: "Behold, I stand at the door and knock. If anyone hears my voice and opens the door, [then] I will enter his house and dine with him, and he with me."

REVELATION 3:20

REFLECTION: At the dawn of each new year, there is a wonderful invitation and promise from our Lord. Every year, Christ offers us an opportunity for a new beginning, a renewed effort in those areas that truly matter. Many people try to make New Year's resolutions: exercising more, spending less money, setting aside more time for family, etc. This age-old custom is a popular expression of Christ's invitation to new life, even though this action is often not taken very seriously. Consider for a moment what makes this so for you.

What if you made only one resolution this year: to accept the Lord's invitation and consciously open the door to his presence each day at the very beginning of your day? Saint Paul says we should pray unceasingly. Let us begin then.

Each morning when you wake up and either jump in the shower, grab your coffee, or fix a bowl of cereal, STOP. Consciously open the door to your heart and let Christ speak to you. Sit across from the table with him for the first five to ten minutes of your day, confident of his promise to be there with you. Do the same thing at night for five to ten minutes. Can you imagine any more important way to begin and end your day? This simple resolution alone, whether you make it now or at the beginning of a new year, has the power to transform your life and will give you the strength to listen and follow the Lord wherever you may go.

QUOTE: *"Unceasing prayer means to have the mind always turned to God with great love, holding alive our hope in him, having confidence in him whatever we are doing and whatever happens to us."*

MAXIMUS THE CONFESSOR

ACTION: Begin today to set a consistent period of time apart each day and be faithful to it for at least one week.

PRAYER: Lord, I know that you always keep your promises. Help me to accept your invitation to daily and consciously welcome your presence in my life. Let this be the one resolution I don't give up on!

LETTING CHRIST IN

SCRIPTURE: "Yet I live, no longer I, but Christ lives in me; insofar as I now live in the flesh, I live by faith in the Son of God who has loved me and given himself up for me."

GALATIANS 2:20

REFLECTION: Have you ever wondered if you are living your life, or merely surviving it? Saint Paul discovered and taught a paradox of our faith. We truly live our life when we let go of it. Discovering our real life allows us to be truly free; this freedom is most radically found, as Saint Paul professes, in the life of Christ Jesus. The heart of the spiritual journey is letting go in order to live a more free and joy-filled life. Yet we live in a culture that conditions us to spend, take, acquire, and self-serve.

To echo Blessed John Paul II, making a choice to follow Christ is the difference between living a life of self-assertion or a life of self-donation. When we assert the self, our spirit is left feeling empty and spiritually tired. When we donate ourselves, our spirit is filled and spiritually energized because our heart is expanded beyond our own ego.

If we are serious about letting Christ, our true life, live in us, then we have to examine those things that crowd him out. God invites us to let Christ dwell in us in order to touch the Christ who lives in everyone. We become the image of Christ for all to see. There is an ancient Hindu saying: *Namaste*, or, "the God in me greets the God in you!"

QUOTE: *"Whatever you possess must not possess you; whatever you own must be under the power of your soul; for if your soul is overpowered by the love of this world's goods, it will be totally at the mercy of its possessions."*

SAINT GREGORY THE GREAT

ACTION: This day, take a moment to ask yourself: Am I allowing Christ to live in me at the surface for all to see? If not, what am I holding onto instead? When you approach another, silently greet the God in them.

PRAYER: Tender God, you gave me your Son that I "might have life and have it more abundantly" (John 10:10). Help me to relinquish my own life that Christ may live and breathe and act in me.

THE VOICE WITHIN

SCRIPTURE: "What is truth?"   JOHN 18:38

REFLECTION: Pilate's question is one we all must wrestle with: What is truth?

Truth for the Christian is not a "what" but a "who." Jesus tells us, "I am the way, the *truth* and the life!" Therefore, it is essential to understand this Christian mystery where truth is not merely an intellectual supposition but a person. God, who created all things out of a lavish love, assumed human flesh in Christ and continually comes to us through the Holy Spirit. The triune God permeates our lives and animates and sustains our very existence, teaching us how to bring our unique gifts to the service of our communities. This expression of the person-hood of God as truth is the meaning of our lives.

But how do we discern and live this mystery of God as "Truth?" As we have said, discernment of any kind is both an internal and external effort. One must be a person of prayer who hears the word and also a person of action who acts on what she hears. How can we tune our ears to hear God's voice, and why should we?

Through God's voice both within the silence of our hearts as well as the voice we find and hear through the events, people and tasks of daily life, God reveals the way we should go. So we must learn to be good listeners: open, docile, and receptive to Yahweh's voice everywhere in the world within and around us.

We often think of prayer as talking to God. While true, it is often more important to still ourselves and listen attentively to God's voice, the deepest truth within us.

QUOTE: *"If, then, you are looking for the way by which you should go, take Christ, because he himself is the way....If you are looking for a goal, hold fast to Christ, because he himself is the truth, where we desire to be."*

SAINT THOMAS AQUINAS

ACTION: As you go about your day, notice the pattern of your thoughts. Do they reflect the truths proposed by the world or the *truth* of the Gospel?

PRAYER: Dearest Lord, give me the strength today to hear your voice deep within, among the many voices clamoring for atten-tion outside of me. Give me the courage to act on what I hear.

MY LIFE IS NOT MY OWN

SCRIPTURE: "Jesus, looking at him, loved him and said to him: 'You are lacking one thing. Go, sell what you have, and give to [the] poor, and you will have treasure in heaven; then come, follow me.'"

MARK 10:21

REFLECTION: I have often thought that we are raised with two very unhelpful myths: that we can do whatever we want when we grow up and that our life is our own. Neither of these teachings could be further from Christ's teaching. What we desire from moment to moment often changes as quickly as the weather. What we want to do may have nothing to do with what God needs from our life for the building of the reign of God on earth. Doing what we want may provide instant gratification, but in order to be fully alive and truly happy we must align our will with that of God.

Why? Because, my dear friends, we have not been made for ourselves and our own passing purposes. God has created us with an eternal purpose. Saint Augustine captured this insight powerfully in the fourth century when he prayed, "Oh Lord, you have made us for yourselves, and our hearts will not rest until they rest in you."

This is the greatest freedom: to be disabused of this notion that this is my life. Our deepest joy acknowledges the truth that my life has been gifted by God and given for a short time. Thus, our lives will someday be returned to God. This is the heart of our sojourn here on this earth: to continually make a return of this gift called life to the one who gave it to me in the first place. In a snapshot, the spiritual life is the loving bestowal of a gift that finds its way back to the one who first lovingly bestowed it.

–BY A.C.W.

QUOTE: *"We do not really belong to ourselves; we belong to the one who redeemed. Our will should always depend on his. For this reason we say in the Lord's Prayer, 'Your will be done.'"*

SAINT BRAULIO

ACTION: Look at your schedule today and reflect on several concrete ways you can give back in the course of this day what has been given to you.

PRAYER: Dear God, remind me today that everything is a gift, neither merited nor entitled. Help me to enjoy in all possible ways, small and great, that I can make a full return of that gift back to you this day.

CLEARING AWAY THE CLUTTER

SCRIPTURE: "For you are a people holy to the LORD, your God; the LORD, your God, has chosen you from all the peoples on the face of the earth to be a people specially his own."

DEUTERONOMY 7:6

REFLECTION: How often do we hear our inmost voice say, I want to become holy or I wish I were holier? The author of Deuteronomy makes clear that we are already sacred and chosen in God's eyes.

At the time when Michelangelo was working on his famous masterpiece David, someone asked him how he created something so beautiful out of a piece of rock. Michelangelo is rumored to have responded, "I didn't create David, he was already there. I just cleared away the junk." And so it is with us and God. God's love is already there inside us beseeching us to be holy as God is holy. God just clears away the layers of junk gathered on the outside that hides our stunning beauty, for we are God's handiwork.

What difference would it make if each morning we got out of bed confident that we were already holy, God's very own, and lived our day out of that belief? I saw a poster recently on a classroom wall that emphatically proclaimed, *God does not create junk!* But we often treat ourselves as though we have doubts. We get down on ourselves, beat ourselves up, and focus on all that we are not rather then on all that we are.

There is "junk" that obscures the beauty of God's holiness in us. It is called sin, and it is an unholy clutter that needs to be cleared away each day. However, clearing away the junk is different than *being* junk, an impossible reality as we are masterpieces made in the image of God, the grand artist of all seen and unseen beauty. But like all art that is not properly taken care of, layers of dirt and grime gradually accumulate over time. Are we open to God clearing away the buildup of that which keeps us from the fullness of life?

QUOTE: *"When we remove all obstacles to his presence he will come, at any hour and moment, to dwell spiritually in our hearts, bringing with him the riches of his grace."*

SAINT CHARLES BORROMEO

ACTION: Today, take an honest look in the mirror and see whose image you really reflect. Clear away the layers that tarnish the primary, divine reflection of God within.

PRAYER: Gracious God, you are the grand artist who images us after yourself. Give us the courage today to own the beautiful piece of art that you have created and to focus on cleaning off any layers of sinful soot that darken your great masterpiece. Help us believe that the clutter of sin, while diminishing the brilliance of your image within us, can never erase it.

ALLOWING CHRIST TO ENTER YOUR LIFE

SCRIPTURE: "I no longer call you slaves, because a slave does not know what his master is doing. I have called you friends, because I have told you everything I have heard from my Father."

JOHN 15:15

REFLECTION: Saint Thomas Aquinas makes the point that while God can certainly be thought of as a loving parent, Christ most wants to relate to us as a friend. Friends share everything with one another: joys and sorrows, strengths and weaknesses, what they are proud of and what they are ashamed of. Friends are vulnerable to one another.

However, Christ's friendship is not intended to be a "greeting-card friendship" that seeks never to challenge for fear of offending the other. True friends call you to something more, to be more than you thought you could be.

They challenge us to not play small with our lives or to settle for mediocrity, especially spiritual mediocrity. This is the purpose of the Church: to bear witness to the one who comes in friendship. And the Church does that by always calling us not to have more but to *be* more. What is the more that you are going to allow Christ, your friend, to call you to this year? Will it be the same old stuff, or will you change your pattern and set out to follow Christ?

Christ promises to be our Savior. Can we stop using other people, things, and adrenaline rushes of various sorts in order to be our own and open ourselves to the real thing: fullness of life? Are you willing to allow Christ to enter your life in any way he pleases and at any moment, including this very moment, hour, or minute? We so often say: I want to be generous, Lord, but on my terms. I want to be different God, but don't ask me to change.

What has to be different to make you more generous? It's time to get off the couch spiritually and make that divine friendship and its spiritual demands for the best we have to offer our priority. Because any friendship that doesn't make demands is not a friendship worth having! It is to our true friends, after all, that we are most accountable.

QUOTE: *"Just as human law aims primarily at friendship between men, so God's law aims primarily at friendship of man for God. But love is based on likeness, and to love God, who is most good, man must become good himself."*

SAINT THOMAS AQUINAS

ACTION: If you and your friend, God, were walking along the beach today, what issue would he hold you accountable for? What would you tell him about that accountability?

PRAYER: Divine friend, I know you call me to something more. It's you speaking to my heart when I feel inside there must be something more than this. Help me not to be afraid of what that more might be. You know me better than I know myself, and friends don't have to be afraid of friends.

THE PRICE IS HIGH

SCRIPTURE: "Whoever loses his life for my sake will find it."

MATTHEW 16:25

REFLECTION: Elizabeth's confidence and conviction in her call to serve God as a consecrated religious had been growing. She believed she was ready to move toward her call, having gained greater reliance on God. She felt great joy and fresh commitment to embrace her call, but at home her readiness was not embraced so eagerly.

In direct proportion to her soaring spirits, her letdown at the reception of this news received by those closest to her was crushing. How could this be? Why were her nearest and dearest the least supportive of her decision. The family could sense her growing "separateness," and this was frightening to them. She was also upset by their reaction. Arguments ensued, and hard words were exchanged. The family discussion came to a dead end.

What was the question Elizabeth needed to ask? What was God saying to her in this desolation? What role does this experience play in her prayer and discernment? Was her longing to be for Christ deeper than the initial resistance of her family to her decision?

At times like this it is important to cultivate an attitude of calm waiting. All things have their time and season. Experiences of consolation and desolation are part of the Christian journey. Patient waiting in prayer and faith is necessary to find peace in God. Listen to the words of Habakkuk: "For the vision is a witness for the appointed time, a testimony to the end; it will not disappoint. If it delays, wait for it, it will surely come, it will not be late" (Habakkuk 2:3).

QUOTE: *"Be faithful to the truth and to its transmission, for truth endures; truth will not go away. Truth will not pass or change."*
POPE JOHN PAUL II (MESSAGE TO THE UNITED NATIONS, 1979)

ACTION: Offer this pain to the one who taught us how to suffer. Ask Mary to teach you how to stand by the cross.

PRAYER: Lord, let me not be afraid of these setbacks on my journey. You know how my heart loves, but my will is in need of some daily courage.

PART V
Signs of a Good Discernment

"Just as when our health is good we can tell the difference between good and bad food by our bodily sense of taste and reach for what is wholesome, so when our mind is strong and free from all anxiety, it is able to taste the riches of divine consolation, and to persevere, through love, the memory of this taste. This teaches us what is best with absolute certainty. As Saint Paul says: 'My prayer is that your love may so increase more and more in knowledge and insight, and so enable you to choose what is best.'"

DIADOCHUS OF PHOTICE

"Oh, God, we were made for you and our hearts will not rest until they rest in You."

SAINT AUGUSTINE OF HIPPO

The common signs of a good discernment are:

1. Action (I am moved to do something).
2. Affirmation (listening and hearing those around us).
3. Seeing the signs God gives us through the people and events we experience in our lives.

Upon reflection, we begin to ask questions such as:

1. Do I have peace once I make my decision? Is my heart at rest?
2. What does my spiritual experience of the discernment process and my prayer life now suggest about my relationship with God?
3. Is there a peaceful resolution even though one cannot know with complete certainty the will of God?

Peace is not a complete absence of fear and nervousness as one makes a leap of faith. Every spiritual path exists with some uncertainties. The question that remains should be: Do we feel God's presence as we make our decision to move in a particular way toward God? Through the gift of peace, Christ affirms our decision.

THE CALL CONFIRMED

SCRIPTURE: "I...chose you and appointed you to go and bear fruit."

JOHN 15:16

REFLECTION: Amelia was living a full life. After completing a degree program in nursing and working as an RN, she had a desire to heal others both physically in healthcare and spiritually through ministry. She worked hard to earn an MA in psychology and had a very successful therapy practice. A generous person, Amelia began to search for the *more* in her life.

Growing up on a military base in Malaysia, her father took his daughters to the far side of the island, where they met amazing women who worked with the poor on farms. With generosity and joyfulness, this group of missionary sisters served the island people. It was this incredible group that she recalled as she pondered the *more* she was desiring. Did God want her to use her nursing and psychology in some form of religious call? After much prayer, discussion, and discernment, God gave Amelia the grace to embrace this missionary call.

As the time approached for Amelia to share this call, she wondered: Who would be the most likely to accept this unexpected turn of her life direction? In the initial stages of discernment she mentioned service to the Church. It fell on deaf ears. After some time, she decided to tell her colleagues. *Their* reaction was very supportive, and they affirmed her decision!

Amelia then told her friends. Life, energy, and generosity roused love and admiration, so it was not surprising that her friends responded with, "You will be a great missionary! We knew you were destined for something great!"

Amelia was blessed with certainty, and her conviction was confirmed when announcing her decision! Confirmation in our decisions, whether for lay ministries, mission work, religious life, marriage—or even selecting whether to go to graduate school or take a particular job—is important. As Amelia experienced from the significant people in her life, we must also look for the support of those around us as we make large and small decisions.

QUOTE: *"It is love alone that gives worth to all things!"*

SAINT TERESA OF ÁVILA

ACTION: Can you recall a time when you were in doubt about a particular decision and were later surprised by God?

PRAYER: May the surrender in faith, hope, and love grace you with the commitment and challenge for the journey. Let us pray that the tender love of Christ embraces you with tranquility.

THE PAINFUL "YES"

SCRIPTURE: "I shall betroth you to myself forever...in faithful love and tenderness."

HOSEA 2:21–22

REFLECTION: Doubts will come and go. The hardest time in Kelly's discernment journey was the Christmas she visited her family the year her sister had her first child. She held the baby in her arms, and the pull on her heartstrings was undeniably painful. Many thoughts went through her mind: *This baby could be mine! The joy and happiness of giving life to another human being will never be my lived experience. How can I move forward as a celibate woman with this harsh reality gathering in my heart and soul?*

These thoughts, questions, and her inner turmoil lasted for weeks. Why me? Why now? First a touch of anger, then denial, and finally fear filled Kelly's heart. The emotional mix of feelings was complicated by the inability to share her dilemma with anyone.

Kelly had an imaginary dialogue with everyone she trusted. Answers did not come. It was only when Kelly sat in silence and waited that a silent voice within spoke to her: "You know that you know *whose* you are." It is crucial to discern what kind of motherhood or fatherhood we are called to embrace. Recently I saw a phrase in an article that went something like, "the call to religious life doesn't remove the desire to be a mother; it transforms it!"

Kelly consulted friends and family for advice in her searching. Some responses that returned to her were: "This life was made for you—it's a good fit. You are, involved, committed and joyful! Do not let this question eradicate years of living and loving the dream." The deepest desire in everyone is to *love,* and a life of chastity is strengthened by an intimate relationship with Christ—the greatest love of all Christian loves!

QUOTE: *"Empty yourself and sit waiting content with the grace of God."*

SAINT ROMUALD

ACTION: Sit and listen as Saint Benedict instructs with "the ears of your heart." Can we live the questions?

PRAYER: Let us pray to entrust this time of discernment to Mary our mother, whose love was spousal, celibate, and fruitful.

WHOSE DREAM ARE YOU FOLLOWING?

SCRIPTURE: "For I know well the plans I have in mind for you—oracle of the LORD—plans for your welfare and not for woe, so as to give you a future of hope."

JEREMIAH 29:11

REFLECTION: Patrick was living the classic American dream that all immigrant parents hope for their children. He was a pre-med student at the top of his class. One weekend he went on a *Come & See* retreat for those discerning a vocation to religious life. He shared no reaction to the weekend except a quiet but polite "no, thank you" and apparently went on with his life.

A month later I saw him while visiting his college. I barely recognized him, so transformed was his whole demeanor. "Patrick, hello, you seem so different, almost like a guy in love," I said. I was about to ask him, "What's her name?" when he said, "Maybe I am [in love], Father, and I didn't know it. I had a breakthrough after I left the *Come & See*. After continually sitting for a while in silence before the Lord each day, as you suggested, it hit me that I needed to follow my dream."

"But Patrick, you *have* a dream, a wonderful dream to be a doctor," I responded.

"No, Father," he responded emphatically, "that's everyone else's dream for me. I think God has a different one for me, and that's the one I am excited to be discovering."

Whose dream are you following?

QUOTE: *"For God has given free will to everyone, and therefore he forces no one but only indicates, calls, persuades."*

SAINT ANGELA MERICI

ACTION: Sit in silent meditation with the different dreams you have had in your life. Let the Lord know the desire of your heart to please him. As you offer this petition, ask for the grace to live with ambiguity, trusting that God knows what he is about in you. Ask for the grace to rest in the unrest.

PRAYER: God of surprises, help me not to daydream about my plans but to God-dream about yours!

GOD SPEAKS IN MY HEART ROOM

SCRIPTURE: "Speak, LORD, for your servant is listening."

1 SAMUEL 3:9

REFLECTION: Michael was six years old when he first told his parents, Angela and John, that he wanted to be a priest when he grew up. He is now twelve and still has not wavered from his "discernment." Why should one so young be taken seriously? One has only to look at the majority of the lives of the saints to recognize that this is classically how God works.

Like the relentless pull of a magnet, God's love often draws us early in our lives. To be sure, Michael is rare in this consistent openness to a calling for one so young. Still, he has already committed himself to prayer, which is a good sign that he should be taken seriously in this early life call.

When I was at lunch with him one day, I told him I had to

give a talk on prayer to some college students and asked that he share with me some tidbits of his prayer life?

He said, "Father, God speaks to me in here," and he pointed to his heart. Each night before bed he prays two decades of the rosary. Sometimes he thinks about the mysteries and of all they reveal about Mary and Jesus' life on earth. Other times he just listens to the rhythm of the words as he speaks them and "it makes me feel good, like a peacefulness." What I was listening to that day was a pre-teen's birth into a new contemplative in the world.

QUOTE: *"But above all preserve peace of heart....In order to preserve it there is nothing more useful than renouncing your own will and substituting for it the will of the divine heart. In this way, he will carry out for us whatever contributes to his glory...."*

SAINT MARGARET MARY ALACOQUE

ACTION: Review the pattern of your daily prayer life. Are you doing the talking while expecting God to do the listening? The birth of the contemplative in you depends less on what you have to say and more on what God wants to speak within you. Be open to God's voice, and try to silence your own will and the chatter that is constantly taking place within.

PRAYER: Gentle Father, the very thing I so deeply hunger for I resist: sitting before you in peaceful silence, wrapped simply in your arms and loving care. Help me to know there is nothing to be afraid of. For my deep hunger to be with you is but a mirror of your deep hunger to be with me.

ARE YOU AT HOME?

SCRIPTURE: "So then you are no longer strangers and sojourners, but you are fellow citizens with the holy ones and members of the household of God, built upon the foundation of the apostles and prophets, with Christ Jesus himself as the capstone. Through him the whole structure is held together and grows into a temple sacred in the Lord; in him you also are being built together into a dwelling place of God in the Spirit."

EPHESIANS 2:19–22

REFLECTION: About two months ago, I was on the second half of a five-mile run when I saw it: the torn wing of a discarded brown cardboard box like millions of others blowing and being kicked around on the streets. As I was running over it, I read it: I went a tenth of a mile more and then turned around to go back and read the makeshift sign for a second time. I began running again, and less than a tenth of mile down the road, turned around and went back a third time. The words struck me: "HI, CAN YOU HELP THE HOMELESS? PLEASE? THANK YOU!"

What am I doing, I thought? This is crazy! But I picked up that "cry for help" and started the two-and-a-half-mile trek back to the priory. Now you can just imagine how self-conscious I was, running in the neighborhood carrying a dirty piece of cardboard trash. But something, or perhaps someone, compelled me.

With all the subtlety of a foghorn, grace stopped me in my

tracks, cut through my usual deafness, and erased my long-distance indifference. Compassion woke me up, and I was struck with the cry of the human beings the sign represented. Perhaps they were and are as discarded and thrown away just as the sign itself.

But even more personally, this declaration of homelessness and the cry for help was mine, too. It echoes in all of us to one degree or another. Homelessness is our universal experience; not so much materially, as in this case, but certainly we each know emotional, spiritual, or psychological homelessness at times.

Homelessness is also a theological reality. The phrase "a pilgrim people" is not mere poetic prose but a statement of our particular plight as human beings. We are all aliens making our way in a foreign land, the world, citizens of another place, as Paul tells us. We have all felt and carry within us that sense of alienation in this desert-wandering of our lives; that sense of not being at home in this world. Who or what is calling us home? What compels us to cry out for help?

–By A.C.W.

QUOTE: "*May the God of love and peace set your hearts at rest and speed you on your journey; may he meanwhile shelter you from disturbance by others in the hidden recesses of his love until he brings you at last into that place of complete plenitude....*"

Saint Raymond of Penyafort

ACTION: In what areas and current circumstances of your life are you feeling alienated or uprooted? Identify and name them before God today.

PRAYER: Heavenly Father, we can feel it in our whole being that we are citizens of another place. We are never entirely at home in this world. We are wired for you, O God. We come from you and one day will return home to you. In the meantime, remind us that you never leave us. In those moments, rescue our awareness from the things below, and restore our entire being to the things above!

GOD ACCOMPANIES US

SCRIPTURE: "Father, they are your gift to me. I wish that where I am they also may be with me, that they may see my glory that you gave me, because you loved me before the foundation of the world."

JOHN 17:24

REFLECTION: At the start of a major discernment effort, one can be full of enthusiasm and clear resolve. We look forward to the journey and feel mentally prepared and ready for the challenge. Further along the road, however, one may begin to feel the natural fatigue and spiritual weariness of the search and perhaps start wondering: Can I make it to the end?

I remember an All-American runner named Nathaniel from Loras College telling me: "Father Wisdom, if you can run seven miles, your body can physically get you the rest of the way. The challenge at that point is not physical, but mental. Are you prepared for the mental warfare? That's what will assault you, tempting you to doubt yourself and give up."

That's true of a committed discernment effort as well. One can encounter all kinds of paralyzing self-doubt, a fear of not being up to the challenge or even worthy of it. The temptation is to give up in midstream. Yet, God does not emotionally jerk us around. He walks the road with us. And just as in a real race where we pause to quench our thirst with water and renew our energy with a healthy snack, God is there to refuel and pump us up, to see us through to the end so that the good work he has begun in us is completed.

To finish the race spiritually in Christ, we have to want what God wants. Once we will something, we need to concretely act on it by taking the life step forward most true to that intention.

We cannot spend our life in discernment, and God does not call us to paralysis. Those who never choose a door from the many before them end up spending their lives in the hallway. When you have discerned God's will as much as you can from the outside, the time comes to discern further internally. The fruit of that discernment is choosing the next step that makes the most sense practically and spiritually.

Though you might feel tired, fatigued, and spent, you can rest with confidence as you stay the course after a decision has been made. It is God, after all, who will carry us over the finish line. For this race is ultimately about one thing: finding rest in God's will and desire for our lives.

QUOTE: *"Exercise self-discipline, for you are God's athlete; the prize is immortality and eternal life, as you well know."*

SAINT IGNATIUS OF ANTIOCH

ACTION: Discuss with a trusted mentor possible next steps. Decide on one, and, if confirmed in prayer, take them.

PRAYER: Shepherd of my soul, I am thirsting for you. Broken down, I am a battlefield of competing desires. Amid the inner warfare, win me over by your indomitable will and become the first place in my heart. You have captured my love. Help me to be all yours now and forevermore.

A DIVINE PURPOSE

SCRIPTURE: "But if any of you lacks wisdom, he should ask God who gives to all generously and ungrudgingly, and he will be given it."

JAMES 1:5

REFLECTION: At a conference that some fellow priests and I attended several years ago, the keynote speaker relayed a dream he had had. He was standing at the foot of the sanctuary of a church as a young boy, staring up at a life-size cross when someone approached him from behind. The person asked a simple question: "What do you want to be when you grow up?"

Without turning around, the boy pointed to the image of the crucified Christ and said: "I want to be as generous as that." This kind of generosity requires a true recognition of one's God-given gifts as something given to us in order to return to God. It means understanding that we are invited to be human agents of a divine purpose.

Sometimes we think we cannot be generous with a vocation unless we clearly understand it. We don't have faith in our calling because we are granted a full understanding of it, but because the one who calls is trustworthy.

God calls us by name, gives us a mission, and provides a road to holiness. It is ours to respond with all the generosity we can muster. Our impetus is the extravagant generosity we find at the foot of the cross. We achieve this as we keep our gaze upon Christ who, in total trust of the Father's will, died with these words on his lips: "Into your hands, I commend my spirit" (Luke 23:46).

QUOTE: *"What, I ask, is more wonderful than the beauty of God.... What desire is as urgent and overpowering as the desire implanted by God in a soul that is completely purified of sin and cries out in its love: I am wounded by love?"*

SAINT BASIL THE GREAT

ACTION: Take fifteen minutes today to meditate upon the cross and its message: Love conquers all. What would a compelling and extravagant generosity of love look like in your own life?

PRAYER: God of abundance, each day is like a blank sheet of paper that I can fill in with acts of generosity and love. Help me to dream big, to let my imagination run wild at all the ways I can be the secret agent of your divine purpose in the world today.

DO NOT MISS YOUR LIFE

SCRIPTURE: "I even consider everything as a loss because of the supreme good of knowing Christ Jesus my Lord. For his sake I have accepted the loss of all things and I consider them so much rubbish, that I may gain Christ and be found in him...."

PHILIPPIANS 3:8–9

REFLECTION: A startling headline on news sites in 2011 was that one of the thirty-two formerly trapped Chilean miners had broken his silence. The television audience was immediately ushered into the living room of one of the rescued miners, who, after a moment or two of speaking, surprised newscasters with a spontaneous urge to go to the beach.

Upon his arrival, this big, tough miner dispenses with his clothes, dances around in a jig of jubilation, likened to that of King David before the Ark of the Covenant, and jumps into the ocean. When he gets out of the water, he suddenly drops to a semi-kneeling, semi-sitting position and, raising his hands to heaven, cries out a prayer, telling God that he will never leave. Then his body shudders with sob after sob.

That image of the rough-and-tumble miner in a humbled heap, overwhelmed with gratitude for the merciful Lord who saved what he had thought lost, powerfully illuminates our faith. Like someone talking tenderly to their beloved, he tells God he will never leave him. Was this an implicit acknowledgement that perhaps he had left God at times in his life? Or was it an explicit awareness that God did not leave him, literally?

The miner's final remarks in the interview did suggest a repentant attitude, resulting in a deep gratitude for letting him live. Why do we worry so much about more money and more things, the miner seemed to ask? Do not waste a second of your life on this. It could all be gone in a moment.

Gratitude and repentance are fruits of the heart's wisdom. To be grateful is to realize all the ways you have been spared because God claims you as his own and calls you to repent in order to know the true happiness of faith. To repent is to change the ways you try to find happiness. Repentance is gratitude's invitation and its only proper response. Gratitude and repentance are like twin engines that propel us forward to an authentic life, as the miner witnessed for us. These are also the indispensable prerequisites for discovering one's vocation!

QUOTE: *"They [Christians] live in their own countries as though they were only passing through....The Christian is to the world what the soul is to the body. As the soul is present in every part of the body, while remaining distinct from it, so Christians are found in all the cities of the world but cannot be identified with the world."*
DIOGNETUS

ACTION: If you were told you had six months to live, how would your priorities change? Review your priorities and determine if you should alter any. Share them with a friend or loved one.

PRAYER: Merciful God, how often I have felt lost and then found by you. Let me be grateful, never taking for granted your promise to always be there for me, no matter what! Let my gratitude cry out as well: "I will never leave you God"...and mean it.

LOVE MAKES DEMANDS

SCRIPTURE: "Trust in the LORD with all your heart, on your own intelligence do not rely; in all your ways be mindful of him, and he will make straight your paths."

PROVERBS 3:5–6

REFLECTION: Nothing stops our Lord dead in his tracks more than our genuine desire to follow him. God will not bypass our heart's deepest desires. God hears us knocking, echoing the earlier divine knock at the home of our hearts, and becomes the lover of our soul.

But when we follow, we may not know what exactly we are getting ourselves into, like the character who lets a guest into his home in C.S. Lewis' parable in *Mere Christianity*. After the guest has been there awhile, his host comes upon renovation plans for a house and realizes it is for his own home! Reviewing them, he is struck with how extensive the new designs are and how much it will alter his current house. Lewis makes the point that the guest, once invited in, is clearly planning on staying and therefore preparing a dwelling that reflects the dignity of his presence.

Not all are open to this kind of guest. For one has to be open as well to being altered and redesigned from within. One has to allow for being radically changed by the experience of peering into the face of the lover of souls and that penetrating look that says: "Give me all of yourself." Love makes demands, so be wary of those loves that do not cost! The only love worth your life is a love that demands of you *e v e r y t h i n g.*

QUOTE: *"Has not God in fact won for himself a claim on all our love...and it is in this vein that he speaks to us: O [my people], consider carefully that I first loved you. You had not yet appeared in the light of day, nor did the world yet exist, but already I loved you. From all eternity I have loved you."*

SAINT ALPHONSUS LIGUORI

ACTION: Read Psalm 139 today and recognize the depth of the Lord's desire for you as you reflect on the care in which God knit you in your mother's womb.

PRAYER: Lover of souls, make of me a worthy dwelling for you. When I resist all the changes you call me to within, be patient with me and help me to be patient with myself.

LET HOLY DESIRES LEAD

SCRIPTURE: "In him we live and move and have our being...."

ACTS 17:28

REFLECTION: The first two small, seemingly unimportant words prayed by the psalmist, "in you," summarize the whole of the spiritual life. They capture the beginning and the end, the place of departure and the point of arrival, the journey and the destination of the path to God. The little words "in you" remind us that nothing occurs outside the providence of God. All is a reflection of the Lord's direct or permissive will (that which is permitted for the greater good).

Even our desire for God is a reflection of Yahweh's initial desire for us. So when you feel the intense hunger for God today, let this little but unfathomable fact put a smile on your face. You could not desire Christ so intensely if he were not desiring you with infinitely more intensity. Your longing for God is but the mirror image of God's longing for you.

Saint Catherine of Siena was known to have made so much progress in her intimacy with our Lord that whenever she made the sign of the cross, she instinctively said: "In the name of the Father and in you and of the Holy Spirit."

QUOTE: *"You called, you shouted, and you broke through my deafness. You flashed, you shone, and you dispelled my blindness You breathed your fragrance on me; I drew in breath and now I pant for you. I have tasted you, now I hunger and thirst for more. You touched me, and I burned for your peace."*

SAINT AUGUSTINE

ACTION: This day, consciously think of your desire for intimacy with the Lord: at work, in front of the copy machine, at the pump in the gas station, or wherever you happen to be. Let that holy desire take the lead in your whole self as you daily live and move and have your being in God.

PRAYER: Lord, you could not love me anymore in the next moment than you do in this moment. Remind me today that my human longing for you is but a reflection of your divine longing for me. Let me live, move, and have my being today in the reflection of your love.